Disney's

SING-ALONG

SONG BOOK

Library of Congress Cataloging-in-Publication Data
Disney's sing-along song book / text by Jim Fanning; introduction by
    Russell Schroeder.
        1 score.
        Melodies with chord symbols.
        ISBN 0-7868-8102-X
        1. Children's songs.   2. Motion picture music—Excerpts, Arranged.
    I. Fanning, Jim.
    M1997.D514   1995   95-5163
                                                         CIP
                                                           M

Designed by Gary Albright
Layout and Production by Nancy Bastan and Cathe Jacobi
Music typesetting by Carolyn Studer
Special thanks to Blake Neely of the Walt Disney Music Company
for his assistance.

10 9 8 7 6 5 4 3 2

Disney's
SING-ALONG
SONG BOOK

TEXT BY JIM FANNING

EDITED AND WITH AN INTRODUCTION
BY RUSSELL SCHROEDER

HYPERION

New York

CONTENTS

INTRODUCTION

From the moment Mickey Mouse first bounced onto movie screens jauntily whistling the popular song "Steamboat Bill," it was evident music would play an important role in the films of the Walt Disney Studio. That fact was dramatically illustrated just a few years later when expert storytelling, breakthrough character animation, and an unforgettable tune ("Who's Afraid of the Big Bad Wolf?") all joined together to create Disney's first hit song, as well as one of the most famous animated cartoons of all time.

Walt Disney once said, "I cannot think of the pictorial story without thinking about the complementary music which will fulfill it." And throughout the thirties the Disney Studio musicians who worked on the Mickey Mouse and Silly Symphonies series continued to use music in innovative and fun ways, sometimes utilizing familiar pieces of music, but more often composing completely original songs and scores.

By 1937 when the first full-length animated feature *Snow White and the Seven Dwarfs* premiered, the Disney music department had become expert at creating memorable songs that not only were an essential part of the character development and storytelling of the films, but also stood on their own as great movie music.

The skillful blending of song and story continued with the majority of the animated features, and also as Disney began producing live-action movies and television shows. When the lessons of successful filmmaking were applied to creating the Disney theme parks, the importance of music was not forgotten, and songs became the driving elements behind some of the parks' most popular attractions.

So, if you are among the millions of people who left the theater humming "A Dream Is a Wish Your Heart Makes" after seeing Cinderella's dreams come true, or emerged from a shallow boat after just completing a colorful around-the-world cruise still singing "It's a Small World," then we are sure you will enjoy the wonderful collection of songs gathered in this book. Their lyrics are fun and romantic, the melodies catchy and memorable. And whether you're seated in front of a piano, in the back seat of a car, or just curled up in your most comfortable chair, you'll enjoy singing them again and again, brightening your day as Snow White once did for us in a darkened theater "With a Smile and a Song."

BAMBI (1942)

With only four songs, *Bambi* is seemingly not much of a musical, especially compared to the tune-filled features that preceded it, such as *Snow White and the Seven Dwarfs* and *Pinocchio*. But music is actually a vital element in *Bambi*, skillfully integrated with the striking imagery and novel storytelling that make this unforgettable film one of Disney's unique animated features.

The poetic, lyrical, yet simply told story of a young deer coming of age, *Bambi* was originally slated to follow *Snow White and the Seven Dwarfs* (1937) as Disney's second animated feature. But the evocative naturalism that Walt Disney wanted for *Bambi* did not come easily or quickly to his animators. Live animals and wildlife film were studied as the Disney artists worked to give the *Bambi* characters both realism and recognizable human emotions. The special challenges of *Bambi* demanded time-consuming experimentation, and the captivating character animation that gave Bambi and Thumper such convincing life could not be rushed. In production for seven years, *Bambi* was finally released in 1942 as Disney's fifth animated feature.

"This is a picture for music...this *Bambi*," Walt Disney told his artists at a story meeting. Dialogue was kept to a minimum; there are only 950 spoken words in the entire film. "We were striving for fewer words," Disney later explained, "because we wanted the action and the music to carry it." The majestic score, running almost nonstop throughout the film, is the audio counterpart of Bambi's magnificent visuals.

Disney had discovered much about the power of music in creating *Fantasia*, and he wanted the *Bambi* score to have as much impact. "Love Is a Song" is a simple yet powerful musical statement that opens *Bambi*, setting the tone for the entire picture and introducing the theme of nature's continuing cycle of life. It was nominated for an Academy Award as Best Song. "There's something in *Bambi*, I think, that will last a long time," observed Walt Disney. Music is a large part of what makes *Bambi* one of the most memorable of his films.

8

LOVE IS A SONG

Words by
Larry Morey

Music by
Frank Churchill

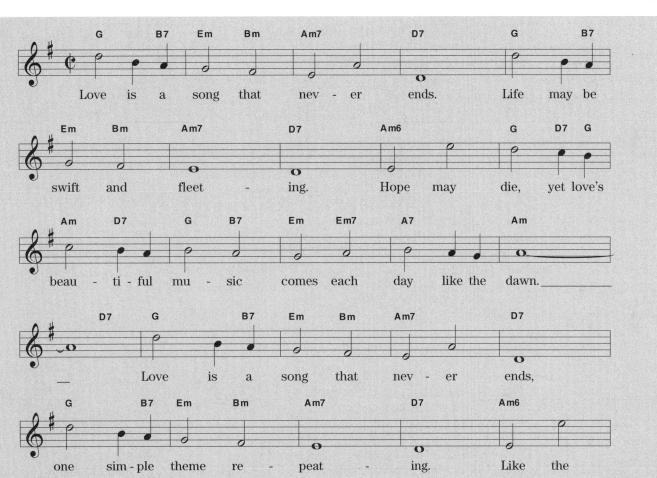

Love is a song that nev-er ends. Life may be swift and fleet-ing. Hope may die, yet love's beau-ti-ful mu-sic comes each day like the dawn. _____ Love is a song that nev-er ends, one sim-ple theme re-peat-ing. Like the

9

voice   of   a   heav - en - ly   choir, _____

love's   sweet   mu - sic   flows

on. _____

SONG OF THE SOUTH (1946)

TWO great storytellers – Uncle Remus and Walt Disney – teamed up for *Song of the South*, a unique hybrid of animation and live action that gave new life to the Southern folk tales of Brer Rabbit, Brer Fox, and Brer Bear preserved by Joel Chandler Harris. "I was familiar with the Uncle Remus tales since boyhood," said Walt Disney. "From the time I began making animation features I have had them in my production plans."

From the outset, Disney pictured Uncle Remus as a live-action performer relating the animated fables. "In James Baskett we found a great actor and the very image of Uncle Remus," he later said of the veteran vaudevillian. "He had, besides the presence and the manner for the role, the eloquent voice needed for the narration."

Baskett also drew on his expertise as a voice artist (he was a regular on radio's "Amos 'n Andy") to play the vocal role of Brer Fox. Animator Marc Davis attested that Baskett "was about the best voice I ever had to work with....He could be hysterical, comic, snide, or mean. The great variety gives inspiration to the physical movement of the character."

Baskett lent his rich, personable style to "Zip-A-Dee-Doo-Dah," one of Disney's most famous songs. A lover of playful new words, Disney is said to have coined the phrase himself and songwriters Ray Gilbert and Allie Wrubel took it from there. The duo's irresistibly optimistic song was at the top of the Hit Parade and won an Oscar as Best Song.

James Baskett's unforgettable portrayal of Uncle Remus has touched generations. The Motion Picture Academy presented the actor with an honorary Oscar "for his able and heart-warming characterization of Uncle Remus, friend and storyteller to the children of the world." With this honor, James Baskett became the first male African-American actor to receive an Academy Award.

FASCINATING FACTS

- The music and characters of *Song of the South* inspired the Splash Mountain attraction at the Disney theme parks.
- Exteriors were filmed on location in Phoenix, Arizona; interiors were shot at the Goldwyn Studios.
- James Baskett's co-star Hattie McDaniel, who plays Aunt Tempy, was the first African-American actress to win an Academy Award (Best Supporting Actress, *Gone With the Wind*).
- The *Song of the South* musical score was nominated for an Oscar.

TRIVIA TEASERS

1. Brer Rabbit gets all tangled up with this fellow who refuses to say hello.
2. Actress Ruth Warrick, who plays Bobby Driscoll's mother in *Song of the South*, became famous for a role on what TV soap opera?
3. You'll find Brer Fox's lair in what locale?
4. What wage does Brer Rabbit promise Brer Bear if he'll take the rabbit's place as a scarecrow?
5. What does Brer Rabbit call home? (HINT: It's where he was "born and bred!")

ANSWERS 1. *The Tar Baby* **2.** "All My Children" **3.** *Chickapin Hill* **4.** *A dollar a minute* **5.** *The Briar Patch*

ZIP-A-DEE-DOO-DAH

Words by
Ray Gilbert

Music by
Allie Wrubel

EV'RYBODY HAS A LAUGHING PLACE

Words by
Ray Gilbert

Music by
Allie Wrubel

FUN AND FANCY FREE (1947)

The "package films"—several animated shorts put together to make a feature-length film—were devised by Walt Disney as a way to keep his studio going immediately after the lean years of World War II without investing time and money in the production of a costly single-story feature. In *Fun and Fancy Free*, Walt Disney brought back Jiminy Cricket, the popular star of *Pinocchio* (1940), to introduce audiences to the charming story of Bongo the Wonder Bear, a little circus star who escapes the Big Top for the wide-open spaces of a magnificent forest.

The package films are unique in their reliance on popular performers of the period, like the Andrews Sisters, Benny Goodman, and Dennis Day, to handle the musical storytelling. *Fun and Fancy Free* was no exception. The "Mickey and the Beanstalk" segment (starring Mickey, Donald, and Goofy in the part traditionally filled by a lad named Jack) is narrated by favorite radio and movie ventriloquist Edgar Bergen, with Charlie McCarthy tossing in irreverent wisecracks just the way he did on the duo's radio show whenever Bergen retold a fairy tale.

When it came to telling the tale of Bongo, Walt Disney had a vocalist in mind, saying, "We'll get the foremost singer of romantic ballads in America." Walt referred to popular radio and recording star Dinah Shore, who ably provided both the narration and the vocalizing for "Bongo." The "Bongo" songs are well suited to Shore's lovely voice and warm personality, especially the lyrical "Lazy Countryside," which musically celebrates the idyllic world of nature opened to Bongo through his newfound freedom.

16

TRIVIA TEASERS

1. What was Cliff Edwards' stage name?
2. According to another *Fun and Fancy Free* song, how do bears like Bongo and his sweetheart show love?
3. What is the name of the big bear who bullies Bongo?
4. On what sort of vehicle does Bongo travel in his new life of freedom?
5. What is the name of Bongo's sweetheart?

ANSWERS
1. Ukulele Ike 2. They "Say It With a Slap" 3. Lumpjaw 4. Unicycle 5. Lulubelle

LAZY COUNTRYSIDE

Words & music
by Bobby Worth

17

LAZY COUNTRYSIDE (CONT'D.)

MELODY TIME (1948)

Ridin' cyclones, shootin' stars and ropin' rustlers by the dozen — that's Pecos Bill, legendary broncbuster born of Texas tall tales. "Pecos Bill," observed Walt Disney, "is a large and important part of our country's heritage and what makes us who we are." The larger-than-life "one-man rodeo" was the natural choice for Disney's first animated tall tale, part of the 1948 feature *Melody Time*.

"Being storytellers ourselves, we've always wanted to portray the deeds of such colorful characters as Johnny Appleseed, Davy Crockett, Paul Bunyan and many others," Disney explained. So when looking for suitable subjects for his animated "package films" of the 1940s, Disney gravitated towards the tall tales. The exaggeration, outrageous humor and all-American high spirits of these wild whoppers made the tall tales the perfect subject for the outsized action possible only in animation.

Disney decreed the story of Pecos Bill be told in song. Songwriters Eliot Daniel and Johnny Lange put Bill's legend into lyric and melody, and Roy Rogers and the Sons of the Pioneers sang the musical tall tale to Disney's youthful stars Bobby Driscoll and Luana Patten. Gathered around a desert campfire, Bobby and Luana find out why coyotes howl at the moon from the smooth Western harmonies of "Pecos Bill" and the wild animated visualizations of this "Western superman."

When Disneyland Park was unveiled in 1955, Pecos Bill held a place of honor in Frontierland. The Golden Horseshoe Saloon was owned and operated by none other than Bill's lady love, Slue Foot Sue, and comedian Wally Boag took on the role of Bill in the Horseshoe's rousing, no-holds-barred finale—all set to the tune of "Pecos Bill."

The Golden Horseshoe Revue earned a top spot in the Guinness Book of World Records as the show with the greatest number of performances in history (nearly 50,000 from 1955 to the show's final curtain call in 1986), a fitting tall tale-type distinction in keeping with the legendary exploits of Pecos Bill, "the rootin'est, tootin'est, shootin'est cowboy to ever ride out of American folklore."

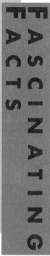

PECOS BILL

Words by
Johnny Lange

Music by
Eliot Daniel

West   of   the   A - la - mo. _____

Additional Lyrics:

2. Once he roped a ragin' cyclone out of nowhere,
    Then he straddled it and settled down with ease,
    And while that cyclone bucked and flitted,
    Pecos rolled a smoke and lit it,
    And he tamed that orn'ry wind down to a breeze.
    refrain

3. Once there was a drought that spread all over Texas
    So to sunny Californy he did go,
    And though the gag is kind a corny
    he brought rain from Californy,
    That's the way we got the Gulf of Mexico.
    refrain

4. Once a band of rustlers stole a herd of cattle
    But they didn't know the herd they stole was Bill's,
    And when he caught them crooked vill'ins
    Pecos knocked out all their fillin's;
    That's the reason why there's gold in them thar hills.
    refrain

5. Pecos lost his way while travlin' on the desert;
    It was ninety miles across the burnin' sand.
    He knew he'd never reach the border
    If he didn't get some water,
    So he got a stick and dug the Rio Grande.
    refrain

6. Now one day Pecos found his fav'rite dogie missin',
    The dogie that was nearest to his heart,
    So then he lassoed all the cattle
    Clear from Texas to Seattle;
    That's the way the Texas round-up got its start.
    refrain

7. While reclinin' on a cloud high over Texas,
    With his gun he made the stars evaporate.
    Then Pecos saw the stars declinin'
    So he left one brightly shinin'
    As the emblem of the
    Lone Star Texas State.
    refrain

SO DEAR TO MY HEART (1949)

Animals, children, trains, and rural America, all favorite things of Walt Disney, all sewn together into a cozy patchwork quilt of a movie called *So Dear to My Heart*. Although a little-known work today, it was one of Walt's personal favorites. "*So Dear* was especially close to me," he once said. "Why, that's the life my brother and I grew up with as kids out in Missouri."

Though Disney used animated segments to illustrate the thoughts and dreams of a young boy named Jeremiah, whose love for a black sheep drives the boy's grandmother to distraction, *So Dear to My Heart* was Disney's most extensive use of live action to date, and he cast the picture with a master's touch. Bobby Driscoll received rave reviews in the role of Jeremiah and character actress Beulah Bondi was the ideal choice for Granny Kincaid.

In his first film, everyone's favorite balladeer, Burl Ives, proved himself an inspired actor as Uncle Hiram, a fact noted by other Hollywood producers.

A collector and performer of authentic American folk songs, Ives' simple but sure performance of "Lavender Blue (Dilly Dilly)" enhances its authentic folk-song ring; the song was adapted from an English folk tune by Eliot Daniel and Larry Morey and garnered an Academy Award nomination.

So Dear to My Heart's atmospheric period detail struck a chord with Walt Disney. As a hobby, he recreated the interior of Granny Kincaid's cabin in miniature, appointing it with rugs, wallpaper, a spinning wheel, even the family Bible. Disney planned on exhibiting the scene—recreating her Granny Kincaid role, Beulah Bondi recorded narration for the exhibit—but soon realized "Granny's Cabin" was too small to be seen by more than a few people at a time. So Disney eventually channeled his ideas, on a larger scale, into Disneyland Park and the charming small-town nostalgia of Main Street, USA.

FASCINATING FACTS

- *So Dear to My Heart* was filmed on location in the San Joaquin Valley, some 250 miles from Hollywood.
- Bobby Driscoll was awarded an honorary Academy Award as Outstanding Juvenile, 1949.
- Bobby Driscoll and his co-star Luana Patten were Disney's first contract players; their Disney debut was in *Song of the South*.
- *So Dear to My Heart* is based on the story *Midnight and Jeremiah*, by novelist Sterling North.

TRIVIA TEASERS

1. What is Uncle Hiram's profession?
2. Where and when is *So Dear to My Heart* set?
3. What is the name of the famous racehorse that Jeremiah so admires?
4. This cartoon bird is an important figure in Jeremiah's scrapbook.
5. In what Disney musical does Burl Ives sing "The Ugly Bug Ball"?

ANSWERS 1. Blacksmith 2. Fulton Corners, Indiana, 1903 3. Dan Patch 4. The Wise Old Owl 5. Summer Magic (1963)

LAVENDER BLUE (DILLY DILLY)

Words by
Larry Morey

Music by
Eliot Daniel

LAVENDER BLUE (DILLY DILLY) (CONT'D.)

"yes," in a pret-ty lit-tle church on a dil-ly, dil-ly day

{you'll / I'll} be wed in a dil-ly, dil-ly dress of lav-en-der

blue, dil-ly, dil-ly, lav-en-der green, Then {I'll / you'll} be

king, dil-ly, dil-ly and {you'll / I'll}

be {my / your} queen. _____

CINDERELLA (1950)

"Ever since *Snow White and the Seven Dwarfs*, I have been eager to make a feature which would possess all of that picture's entertainment qualities and have the same worldwide appeal," Walt Disney said in introducing *Cinderella*, his version of the world's most famous fairy tale. In recapturing the *Snow White* magic, Walt knew the importance of song, and he turned to a fresh source of inspiration: New York's Tin Pan Alley.

Singer Perry Como had a hit with the catchy novelty tune "Chi-Baba Chi-Baba," and when Disney discovered the song was composed by Mack David, Al Hoffman, and Jerry Livingston, the New York composers found themselves at a command performance. "We played a medley of our songs for Walt, but you could see that he was more interested in 'Chi-Baba,'" remembered Jerry Livingston. "I think then he had in mind something similar for the Fairy Godmother's magic scene. But he didn't want something ordinary like 'Ali-Kazam.'"

The Tin Pan Alley trio was enlisted to write the *Cinderella* songs, including the far-from-ordinary "Bibbidi-Bobbidi-Boo," providing the Fairy Godmother with some very special magic words, "believe it or not," while also musically conveying her jovial, generous character.

But the heartfelt ballad "A Dream Is a Wish Your Heart Makes" was the first *Cinderella* song created by the songwriters. "When we went to play it for Walt, he simply said, 'That'll work,' and asked us to have a demo record made," revealed Livingston. "We weren't sure who to use for the vocal, since we were new to Hollywood. Finally Mack remembered that Ilene Woods, a singer we knew from the 'Hit Parade,' was now living in Hollywood, so we used her. When Walt heard her voice, he got excited....The next thing we knew, she was hired for the voice of Cinderella."

Woods' lovely vocalization of "A Dream Is a Wish Your Heart Makes" helped make it a hit, sharing the two top spots on the "Hit Parade" with "Bibbidi-Bobbidi-Boo."

FASCINATING FACTS

- Eleanor Audley, the voice of Cinderella's stepmother, later gave voice to another Disney villainess: Maleficent in *Sleeping Beauty* (1959).
- At Walt Disney's suggestion, animator Ward Kimball used his own calico cat as the model for the nasty Lucifer.
- "Bibbidi-Bobbidi-Boo" was nominated for an Academy Award as Best Song; the *Cinderella* score was nominated for Best Scoring of a Musical Picture.

TRIVIA TEASERS

1. Cinderella numbers a dog and a horse among her animal friends. Can you name them?
2. What is Cinderella's stepmother's name?
3. Whose royal duty is it to try the glass slipper on every maiden in the land?
4. What veteran Disney sound effects artist is given credit for voicing the *Cinderella* mice Gus and Jaq? (HINT: He was also voicing another famous Disney mouse by this time.)
5. Why is the King so anxious for his son, Prince Charming, to marry?

ANSWERS: *1. Bruno and Major 2. Lady Tremaine 3. The Grand Duke 4. Jimmy Macdonald 5. The King wants grandchildren.*

A DREAM IS A WISH YOUR HEART MAKES

Words & music
by Mack David,
Al Hoffman &
Jerry Livingston

how your heart is griev-ing, if you keep on be-liev-ing, the dream that you

wish will come true. _____

BIBBIDI-BOBBIDI-BOO (THE MAGIC SONG)

Words & music
by Mack David,
Al Hoffman &
Jerry Livingston

30

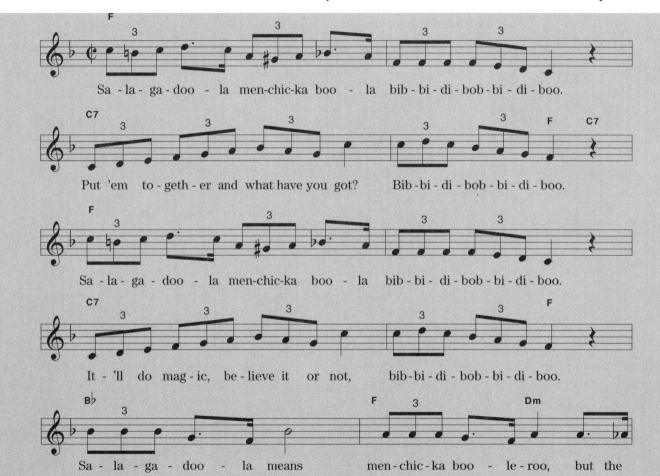

thing - a - ma - bob   that does   the job   is   bib - bi - di - bob - bi - di - boo.

Sa - la - ga - doo - la men-chic-ka boo - la   bib - bi - di - bob - bi - di - boo.

Put 'em   to-geth - er and what have you got?   Bib-bi-di - bob - bi - di, bib - bi - di - bob - bi - di,

bib - bi - di - bob-bi - di - boo!

ALICE IN WONDERLAND (1951)

"Curiouser and curiouser!" exclaimed Alice, and it's a fitting comment on the wildly wacky fantasy world of Disney's *Alice in Wonderland*. Walt had long been intrigued by Lewis Carroll's surreal classic, but it took many years of trying to get a handle on Carroll's literary madness before Walt could put his animated *Alice* into production. Veteran songwriters Sammy Fain and Bob Hilliard were brought in to work with the Disney staff, contributing a collection of tunes ranging from quaint to crazy.

Sammy Fain recalled composing "I'm Late," the frantic theme of the frazzled White Rabbit: "The original version was somewhat different, not as hurried. We had played it for Walt and he liked it. But that night I kept thinking about it and finally wrote out a second version. The next day I got in to see Walt and he was delighted. There are few studios I know of where you could get in to see the top man and have him change his mind on a song." The White Rabbit, who served as an important link throughout the episodic storyline, was voiced by one of Disney's favorite vocal artists, Bill Thompson.

Alice in Wonderland's highlight is the Mad Tea Party, enlivened by the comic vocalizations of Ed Wynn and Jerry Colonna. But as *Alice* was being developed, the film's creators found the sequence a challenge. Jerry Livingston of the *Cinderella* songwriting team of David, Hoffman, and Livingston remembered that Walt Disney "asked us to give it some thought even though we weren't on the picture. Here was a ten-to fifteen-minute scene that they still didn't know quite how to handle." Finally, Mack David latched onto the "unbirthday" idea from Humpty Dumpty in Carroll's *Through the Looking Glass*. "Since there are 364 unbirthdays each year," concluded Livingston, "it was a perfect reason for a mad tea party."

TRIVIA TEASERS

1. What is the name of Alice's cat?
2. What happens to Alice when she sips from the bottle that says "Drink Me"?
3. What is the Queen of Hearts' favorite game?
4. Name the mysterious forest where Alice becomes lost.
5. Who is asleep in the teapot at the Mad Tea Party?

ANSWERS 1. Dinah 2. She shrinks 3. Croquet played with flamingos and hedgehogs as mallets and balls 4. Tulgey Wood 5. The Dormouse

I'M LATE

Words by
Bob Hilliard

Music by
Sammy Fain

I'm late, I'm late for a ver-y im-por-tant date. No time to say hel - lo, good - bye, I'm late, I'm late, I'm late, I'm late and when I wave, I lose the time I save. My fuz-zy ears and whis - kers took me too much time to shave. I run and then I

33

hop, hop, hop, I wish that I could fly. There's dan - ger if I

dare to stop and here's the rea - son why, (you see) I'm o - ver -

due, I'm in a rab - bit stew. Can't e - ven say good -

bye, hel - lo, I'm late, I'm late, I'm late.

THE UNBIRTHDAY SONG

Words & music
by Mack David,
Al Hoffman &
Jerry Livingston

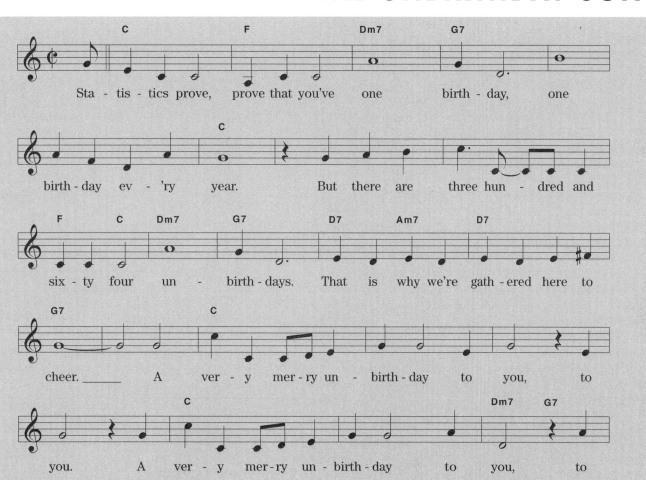

35

you. It's great to drink to some-one and I guess that you will do. A ver - y mer - ry un - birth - day to you.____

Additional Lyrics:

A very merry unbirthday to us, to us.
A very merry unbirthday to us, to us.
If there are no objections let it be unanimous.
A very merry unbirthday to us.

A very merry unbirthday to me. To who?
A very merry unbirthday to me. To you?
Let's all congratulate me with a present, I agree.
A very merry unbirthday to me.

A very merry unbirthday to all, to all.
A very merry unbirthday to all, to all.
Let's have a celebration, hire a band and rent a hall.
A very merry unbirthday to all.

PETER PAN (1953)

"Next to *Snow White*, I cared most for *Peter Pan*," Walt Disney once said, while reminiscing about a road company production of the stage version of *Peter Pan* he had seen in Marceline, Missouri. "It took most of the contents of two toy savings banks to buy tickets, but my brother Roy and I didn't care. For two hours we lived in Never Land with Peter and his friends. I took many memories away from the theatre with me, but the most thrilling of all was the vision of Peter flying through the air."

That high-flying vision was tailor-made for animation. "When I began producing cartoons, *Peter Pan* was high on my list of subjects," Disney said. In fact, Disney acquired screen rights in 1939. By the early 40s, conceptual art, character models, storywork, and music were developed, including "Never Smile at a Crocodile," with a melody by veteran Disney staffer Frank Churchill.

Even so, it was years before Walt could put *Peter Pan* into full production, and audiences had to wait until 1953 to see the grinning, green crocodile the song warned them about. Though the words are never actually sung in the film itself (the song is heard as a musical theme for the tick-tocking croc), the clockwork rhythm and the tricky lyrics by Jack Lawrence have made "Never Smile at a Crocodile" a popular novelty tune—one of the many enduring legacies of Walt Disney's version of *Peter Pan*.

Peter Pan became the second Disney feature to contain songs by Sammy Fain. The talented tunesmith was equally at home providing melodies for the Never Land Indians to sing, the raucous pirates to chant, or for helping us to fly to a magical island with a boy who refused to grow up and his lucky companions.

FASCINATING FACTS

- In his last Disney role, Bobby Driscoll gave voice to Peter Pan.
- Kathryn Beaumont, the voice of Alice in Wonderland, is also the voice of Wendy.
- Tinker Bell went on to become the symbol of the Disney TV show, opening each episode with a wave of her wand, and she soars across the Disneyland and Walt Disney World Magic Kingdoms to start the spectacular Fantasy in the Sky fireworks shows.

TRIVIA TEASERS

1. On what famous London landmark do Peter Pan and the Darling children take a mid-flight break during their journey to Never Land?
2. Where is Pan's hideout?
3. What "gift" from Captain Hook almost finishes off Peter?
4. Peter is looking for this when he flies into the Darling nursery.
5. What is distinct about the Lost Boy Raccoon Twins' way of speaking?

ANSWERS 1. Big Ben 2. Under Hangman's Tree 3. A bomb 4. His shadow 5. Their dialogue is the same, but one is always just a few beats behind the other.

YOU CAN FLY! YOU CAN FLY! YOU CAN FLY!

Words by
Sammy Cahn

Music by
Sammy Fain

38

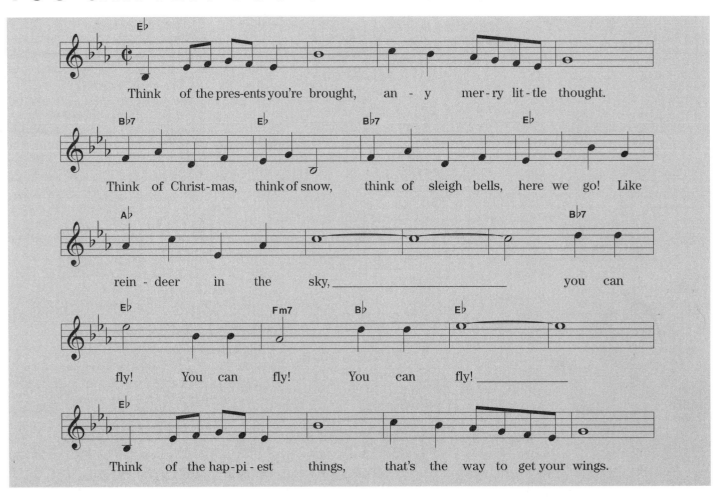

Think of the pres-ents you're brought, an - y mer - ry lit - tle thought.

Think of Christ-mas, think of snow, think of sleigh bells, here we go! Like

rein - deer in the sky, _____ you can

fly! You can fly! You can fly! _____

Think of the hap-pi - est things, that's the way to get your wings.

dust is a pos-i-tive must! _____ When there's a smile in your

heart there's no bet-ter time to start. It's a ver-y sim-ple plan.

You can do what bird-ies can; at least it's worth a try. _____

___ You can fly! You can

fly! You can fly! _____

NEVER SMILE AT A CROCODILE

Words by
Jack Lawrence

Music by
Frank Churchill

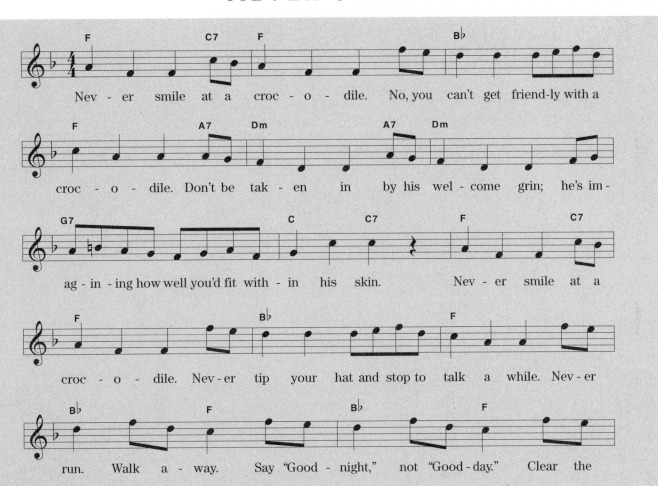

Nev - er smile at a croc - o - dile. No, you can't get friend-ly with a croc - o - dile. Don't be tak - en in by his wel - come grin; he's im - ag - in - ing how well you'd fit with - in his skin. Nev - er smile at a croc - o - dile. Nev - er tip your hat and stop to talk a while. Nev - er run. Walk a - way. Say "Good - night," not "Good - day." Clear the

41

aisle and nev - er smile at Mis - ter Croc - o - dile.

YOUR MOTHER AND MINE

Words by
Sammy Cahn

Music by
Sammy Fain

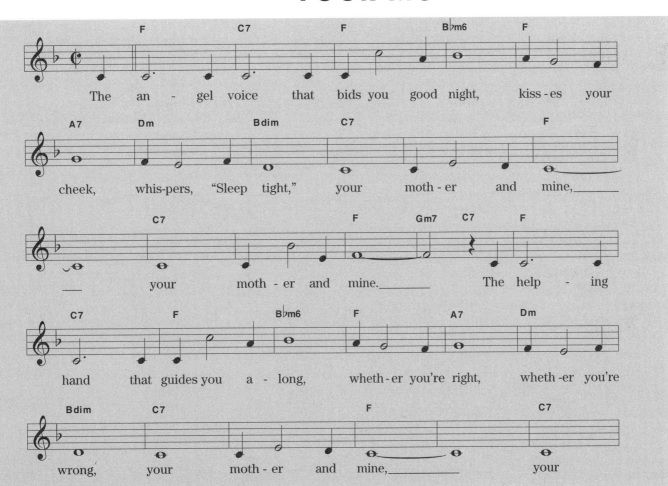

The an - gel voice that bids you good night, kiss-es your cheek, whis-pers, "Sleep tight," your moth - er and mine,_____ your moth - er and mine._____ The help - ing hand that guides you a - long, wheth-er you're right, wheth-er you're wrong, your moth - er and mine,_____ your

YOUR MOTHER AND MINE (CONT'D.)

moth - er   and   mine._____   What   makes   moth - ers

all   that   they   are?   Might   as   well   ask,   "What makes   a

star?"   Ask   your   heart   to   tell you   her   worth;

your   heart   must   say,   "Heav - en   on   earth,   an - oth - er

word   for   di - vine," _____   your   moth - er   and   mine.

DAVY CROCKETT (1954)

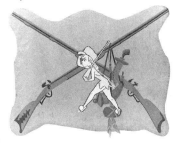

A trailblazer in life and legend, Davy Crockett also blazed a trail in the new medium of television when Walt Disney introduced the story of the frontiersman on his "Disneyland" TV show. Designed to publicize Disney's burgeoning Magic Kingdom in Anaheim, the "Disneyland" series was also a showcase for Disney programming old and new. Among the new for the first season was the three-part story of Davy Crockett.

Walt cast newcomer Fess Parker as Davy and showbiz veteran Buddy Ebsen as sidekick Georgie Russel, and the three episodes were filmed on location in North Carolina and Tennessee. "Walt needed what I call a little 'throwaway' tune that would bridge the time gaps in the story," recalled Disney staff composer George Bruns. "I threw together the melody line and chorus in about 30 minutes." "Davy Crockett" screenwriter Tom Blackburn was pressed into writing the lyrics, though he protested he'd never written a song in his life. But Disney was pleased. "These lyrics are important," he commented at an editing meeting. "They help to keep the story moving."

When "Davy Crockett, Indian Fighter," the first installment of the trilogy, aired, the stampede for the song started. Reflecting the spectacular popularity of the three Davy Crockett shows—it's estimated over 90 million people viewed the original broadcasts—"The Ballad of Davy Crockett" skyrocketed to the top of the charts and spent six months on the Hit Parade. The recording sold 10 million copies, the fastest-selling record in history. "It certainly took everybody at the Studio by surprise," admitted Bruns. "The irony of it was that most people thought it was an authentic folk song that we had uncovered and updated."

Walt Disney brought back Davy the following TV season for "Davy Crockett's Keelboat Race" and "Davy Crockett and the River Pirates," complete with new lyrics for "The Ballad of Davy Crockett."

45

FASCINATING FACTS

- Since "The Ballad of Davy Crockett" was intended to tell Davy's story, it had 120 lines in 20 stanzas and additional stanzas for the two "The Legend of Davy Crockett" episodes that aired in the second season of "Disneyland."
- Walt Disney screened the sci-fi movie *Them!* because he was considering James Arness for the role of Davy. But when he saw bit player Fess Parker, Walt said, "That's Davy Crockett!" (James Arness went on to play Marshall Dillon on TV's "Gunsmoke.")

TRIVIA TEASERS

1. What character actor, who was also the voice of Captain Hook in *Peter Pan*, played the gambler Thimblerig?
2. Davy served under this general who went on to become President of the United States.
3. What was Davy Crockett's motto?
4. What did Davy call his rifle?
5. What was the name of Davy's wife?
6. What song was created when George Bruns set Davy Crockett's own words to music?

ANSWERS 1. Hans Conried 2. Andrew Jackson 3. "Be sure you're right, and then go ahead." 4. Old Betsy 5. Polly 6. "Farewell"

THE BALLAD OF DAVY CROCKETT

Words by
Tom Blackburn

Music by
George Bruns

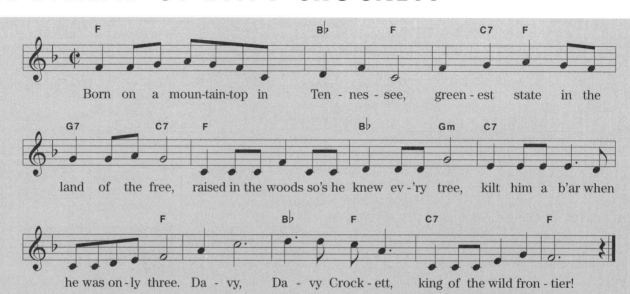

Born on a moun-tain-top in Ten - nes - see, green - est state in the land of the free, raised in the woods so's he knew ev -'ry tree, kilt him a b'ar when he was on - ly three. Da - vy, Da - vy Crock - ett, king of the wild fron - tier!

Additional Lyrics:

2. In eighteen-thirteen the Creeks uprose,
Addin' redskin arrows to the country's woes.
Now, Injun fightin' is somethin' he knows,
So he shoulders his rifle an' off he goes.
Davy, Davy Crockett, the man who don't know fear!

3. Off through the woods he's a-marchin' along,
Makin' up yarns an' a-singin' a song,
Itchin' fer fightin' an' rightin' a wrong,
He's ringy as a b'ar an' twict as strong.
Davy, Davy Crockett, the buckskin buccaneer!

4. Andy Jackson is our gen'ral's name,
His reg'lar soldiers we'll put to shame.
Them redskin varmints us Volunteers'll tame,
'Cause we got the guns with the sure-fire aim.
Davy, Davy Crockett, the champion of us all!

5. Headed back to war from the ol' home place,
But Red Stick was leadin' a merry chase,
Fightin' an' burnin' at a devil's pace
South to the swamps on the Florida Trace.
Davy, Davy Crockett, trackin' the redskins down!

6. Fought single-handed through the Injun War
    Till the Creeks was whipped an' peace was in store.
    An' while he was handlin' this risky chore,
    Made hisself a legend for evermore.
    Davy, Davy Crockett, king of the wild frontier!

7. He give his word an' he give his hand
    That his Injun friends could keep their land.
    An' the rest of his life he took the stand
    That justice was due every redskin band.
    Davy, Davy Crockett, holdin' his promise dear!

8. Home fer the winter with his family,
    Happy as squirrels in the ol' gum tree,
    Bein' the father he wanted to be,
    Close to his boys as the pod an' the pea.
    Davy, Davy Crockett, holdin' his young 'uns dear!

9. But the ice went out an' the warm winds came
    An' the meltin' snow showed tracks of game.
    An' the flowers of Spring filled the woods with flame,
    An' all of a sudden life got too tame.
    Davy, Davy Crockett, headin' on West again!

10. Off through the woods we're ridin' along,
    Makin' up yarns an' singin' a song.
    He's ringy as a b'ar an' twict as strong,
    An' knows he's right 'cause he ain' often wrong.
    Davy, Davy Crockett, the man who don't know fear!

11. Lookin' fer a place where the air smells clean,
    Where the trees is tall an' the grass is green,
    Where the fish is fat in an untouched stream,
    An' the teemin' woods is a hunter's dream.
    Davy, Davy Crockett, lookin' fer Paradise!

12. Now he's lost his love an' his grief was gall,
    In his heart he wanted to leave it all,
    An' lose himself in the forests tall,
    But he answered instead his country's call.
    Davy, Davy Crockett, beginnin' his campaign!

13. Needin' his help, they didn't vote blind.
    They put in Davy 'cause he was their kind,
    Sent up to Nashville the best they could find,
    A fightin' spirit an' a thinkin' mind.
    Davy, Davy Crockett, choice of the whole frontier!

14. The votes were counted an' he won hands down,
    So they sent him off to Washin'ton town
    With his best dress suit still his buckskins brown,
    A livin' legend of growin' renown.
    Davy, Davy Crockett, the Canebrake Congressman!

15. He went off to Congress an' served a spell,
    Fixin' up the Gover'ments an' laws as well,
    Took over Washin'ton so we heered tell
    An' patched up the crack in the Liberty Bell.
    Davy, Davy Crockett, seein' his duty clear!

16. Him an' his jokes travelled all through the land,
An' his speeches made him friends to beat the band.
His politickin' was their favorite brand
An' everyone wanted to shake his hand.
Davy, Davy Crockett, helpin' his legend grow!

17. He knew when he spoke he sounded the knell
Of his hopes for White House an' fame as well.
But he spoke out strong so hist'ry books tell
An' patched up the crack in the Liberty Bell.
Davy, Davy Crockett, seein' his duty clear!

18. When he come home, his politickin' done,
The western march had just begun,
So he packed his gear an' his trusty gun,
An' lit out grinnin' to follow the sun.
Davy, Davy Crockett, leadin' the pioneer!

19. He heard of Houston an' Austin an' so,
To the Texas plains he jest had to go,
Where Freedom was fightin' another foe,
An' they needed him at the Alamo.
Davy, Davy Crockett, the man who don't know fear!

20. His land is biggest an' his land is best,
From grassy plains to the mountain crest,
He's ahead of us all meetin' the test,
Followin' his legend into the West.
Davy, Davy Crockett, king of the wild frontier!

LADY AND THE TRAMP (1955)

Disney went to the dogs when he unleashed *Lady and the Tramp*, a romantic period piece about two pooches who find true love despite differences in pedigree. Originally the classy Lady, who was created in the late 1930s, was to be the solo star, but when Walt read a story by Ward Greene about a carefree mutt, he encouraged the author to team up the two dogs in a new story so Disney could produce this "pet project" as a full-length feature.

In the 1950s the project continued to evolve with the signing of the top-of-the-charts recording artist Peggy Lee as the voice of Lady. Not only a sensuous songstress, but also a talented lyricist, Lee spotted story points for songs. Soon, Walt cast Barbara Luddy as Lady, and appointed Lee to write all of the picture's tunes with composer Sonny Burke.

Walt Disney suggested the scene starring the sneaky Siamese cats be played out in song. Lee and Burke cooked up the Orientally oriented "The Siamese Cat Song." Lee made a demo where she dubbed over her own voice for a duet effect. Upon hearing the test, a delighted Walt Disney insisted that Lee provide the voices of both Siamese "twins," Si and Am.

Something lyrical was needed for Lady and Tramp's candlelight dinner of spaghetti and meatballs. Lee and Burke concocted an Italian-flavored love song so Tony, the romantic restaurateur, and Joe, the cook, could serenade the canines, who find themselves with a serious case of puppy love. The ballad "Bella Notte" sets the scene for one of the most memorable moments in movie history.

Since *Lady and the Tramp* was not based on a story already familiar to the movie-going public, Walt introduced the movie's storyline and its canine stars via episodes of his new "Disneyland" television show. The strategy paid off: *Lady and the Tramp* became one of the Studio's most popular features during its initial release and remains a favorite to this day.

TRIVIA TEASERS

1. What are the names of Lady's doting humans?
2. Name the visiting relative who owns Si and Am.
3. *Lady and the Tramp* opens and closes during which holiday season?
4. Tramp tricks what kind of animal into gnawing off Lady's muzzle?
5. At story's end Lady and Tramp are the proud parents of five puppies. What name was given to their son in comic stories?

ANSWERS 1. Jim Dear and Darling 2. Aunt Sarah 3. Christmas 4. A beaver 5. Scamp

49

THE SIAMESE CAT SONG

**Words & music
by Peggy Lee
& Sonny Burke**

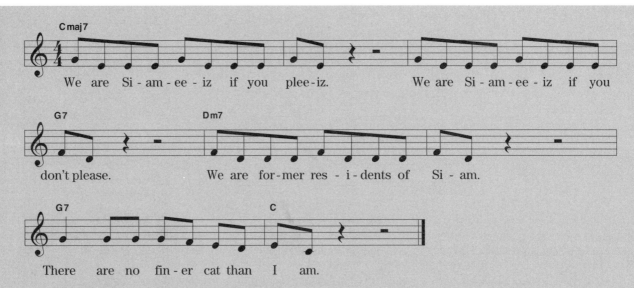

We are Si - am - ee - iz if you plee - iz. We are Si - am - ee - iz if you don't please. We are for - mer res - i - dents of Si - am. There are no fin - er cat than I am.

Additional Lyrics:

2. We are Siamese with very dainty claws,
   Please observing paws containing dainty claws.
   Now we lookin' over our new domicile,
   If we like we stay for maybe quite a while.

3. Who is that who's living in that wire house?
   It must be a bird because it's not a mouse.
   If we sneakin' up upon it carefully,
   There will be some bird for you and some for me.

4. Do you seeing that thing swimmin' 'round and 'round?
   Maybe we could reaching in and make it drown.
   If we sneakin' up upon it carefully,
   There will be a head for you, a tail for me.

5. Do you hear what I hear? A baby cry!
   Where we finding baby, there are milk nearby.
   If we look in baby buggy, there could be
   Plenty milk for you. *SPOKEN: (And also some for me.)*

BELLA NOTTE

**Words & music
by Peggy Lee
& Sonny Burke**

52

make that diz - zy climb. For this _____ is the night ____ and the

heav - ens are right ____ on this love - ly bel - la not - te.

Additional Lyrics:

This is the night,
It's a beautiful night,
And we call it bella notte.
Look at the skies,
They have stars in their eyes
On this lovely bella notte.
Side by side with your loved one,
You'll find enchantment here.
The night will weave its magic spell
When the one you love is near.
For this is the night
And the heavens are right
On this lovely bella notte.

53

THE MICKEY MOUSE CLUB (1955)

Having caused a sensation with his "Disneyland" TV program, Walt decided to create a television show especially for children—the first Disney project produced expressly for kids. Walt wanted his TV club to make every viewer feel "as welcome as can be," so who better to serve as the club's leader than Mickey Mouse himself?

As early as summer 1954, Disney was generating ideas for the proposed show, including a "club song." Jimmie Dodd, a personable composer and performer was given the assignment of creating the club's theme song, and was also signed to host "The Mickey Mouse Club." "Children just seem to take to me and I to them," he explained. "Walt noticed and that's how I became the emcee and song leader for the Mouseketeers."

Walt Disney saw the Club as a vehicle for child performers. "Ordinary kids" was what Walt wanted, and 24 "ordinary" but talented children were handpicked to sing, dance, and smile their hearts out on national TV. Disney himself dubbed the young performers "Mouseketeers."

"The Mickey Mouse Club" premiered on ABC on October 3, 1955, opposite the reigning kiddie show of the day, NBC's "Howdy Doody." It was no contest; three-quarters of the nation's TV sets tuned in as millions of children made a daily ritual of joining Annette, Tommy, Darlene, Cubby, and the other Mouseketeers for Disney cartoons, music, sketches and serials (like "Spin and Marty").

Jimmie Dodd's club song, "Mickey Mouse March," became an anthem with its unforgettable M-I-C-K-E-Y M-O-U-S-E chant. The fan letters that poured in at a rate of over 7,000 a month requested copies of the "March" above anything else.

Even after "The Mickey Mouse Club" ended its four-year run, retiring as the most-watched network children's TV show ever, "Mickey Mouse March" remained a hit. The song stands today as a musical tribute to Walt Disney's first and favorite star.

54

TRIVIA TEASERS

1. Who jealously squawked his own name during the "Mickey Mouse March"?
2. What was Friday called on "The Mickey Mouse Club"?
3. Who was Cubby frequently paired with in songs and sketches?
4. What Disney character hosted such educationally entertaining segments as "I'm No Fool" and "You–The Human Animal"?
5. What magic incantation did the Mouseketeers intone to conjure up a Disney cartoon?

ANSWERS 1. Donald Duck 2. Talent Roundup Day 3. Karen 4. Jiminy Cricket 5. "Meeseka Mooseka Mouseketeer, Mousekartoon time now is here."

MICKEY MOUSE MARCH

Words & music
by Jimmie Dodd

55

MICKEY MOUSE MARCH (CONT'D.)

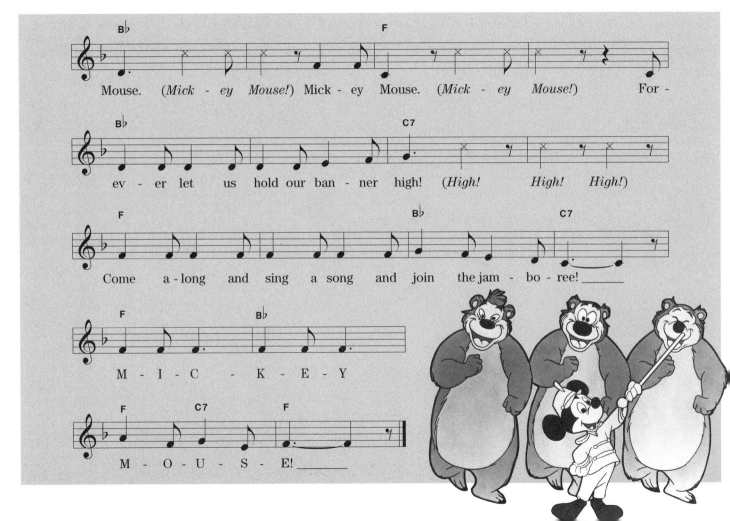

Mouse. (*Mick - ey Mouse!*) Mick - ey Mouse. (*Mick - ey Mouse!*) For -

ev - er let us hold our ban - ner high! (*High! High! High!*)

Come a - long and sing a song and join the jam - bo - ree!

M - I - C - K - E - Y

M - O - U - S - E!

ANNETTE

Words & music
by Jimmie Dodd

Who's the lit - tle la - dy who's as dain - ty as a dream? Who's the one you can't for -

get? I'll give you just three guess-es; An - nette! An-nette! An - nette!

When she dan-ces on her toes, she dan-ces in your heart with her pret - ty pir - ou -

ette. Each lit - tle move ex-pres-ses An - nette! An-nette! An - nette!

Tho' she's just a cute pre - teen - er, And her fa-ther's pride, and Moth - er's joy.

There will come a day they'll give An-nette a-way to the world's luck-i-est

boy! Ask the birds, and ask the bees, and ask the stars a-bove

who's their fav-'rite sweet bru-nette; you know, each one con-

fess-es: An-nette! An-nette! An-nette!

A Day in the Life of Donald Duck (1956)

Donald Duck was an overnight success. Since he made his first appearance, all fury and feathers, in 1934 with that instantly identifiable ducky voice, Donald has been an audience favorite, even rivaling the popularity of Mickey Mouse. With 128 starring-role cartoons, one Oscar-winner and 11 Academy Award-nominated films to his credit, it's no wonder Walt Disney's webfooted star was spotlighted in many episodes of the Disney TV program, including "At Home with Donald Duck" (1956), "Donald's Weekend" (1958), "This Is Your Life, Donald Duck" (1960) and "Inside Donald Duck" (1961). One of the most fascinating of the TV programs was "A Day in the Life of Donald Duck," an intimate "duckumentary" on a typical work day in this Hollywood star's glamorous life. In a truly unique sequence, Donald becomes furious over some fan mail complaining about his unintelligible speech, so he summons to his Studio office his "voice" Clarence Nash, and a duel of "Duck-speak" ensues.

This special show called for a song—after all, Mickey had his own theme, why shouldn't Donald? So Jimmie Dodd, head Mouseketeer and composer of the "Mickey Mouse March," wrote a ducky ditty for Donald. "Quack! Quack! Quack! Donald Duck" was performed by Dodd and the Mouseketeers as a salute to everyone's favorite quacker.

As "A Day in the Life of Donald Duck" amply proved, Donald is a duck whose fury and foibles make him all too human—and lovable. As Walt Disney once observed: "[Donald] is a very outrageous fellow, with bad manners and a worse temper, and everyone is very fond of him, including me."

59

TRIVIA TEASERS

1. In what 1934 Silly Symphony did Donald make his screen debut?
2. According to *Donald Gets Drafted* (1942), what is Donald's middle name?
3. In what cartoon did Huey, Dewey, and Louie first darken Donald's doorway?
4. Donald was officially and honorably discharged from which branch of the military in 1984?
5. In the 1934 Mickey Mouse cartoon *Orphan's Benefit*, Donald displays what personality trait for the first time?

ANSWERS *1. The Wise Little Hen 2. Fauntleroy 3. Donald's Nephews (1938) 4. The Army 5. His temper*

QUACK! QUACK! QUACK! DONALD DUCK

Words & Music
by Jimmie Dodd

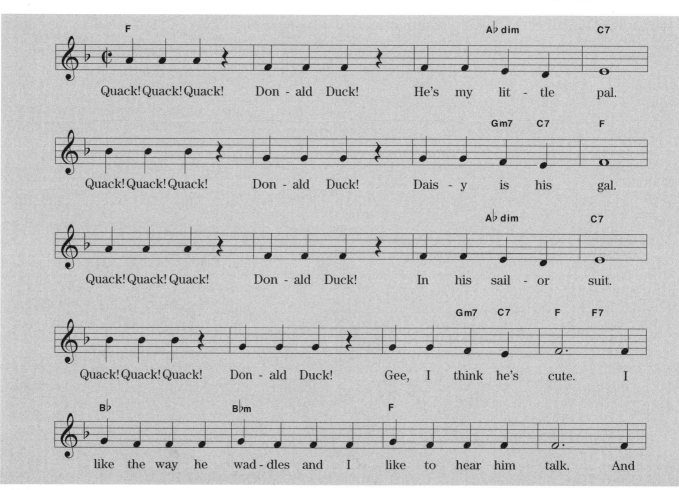

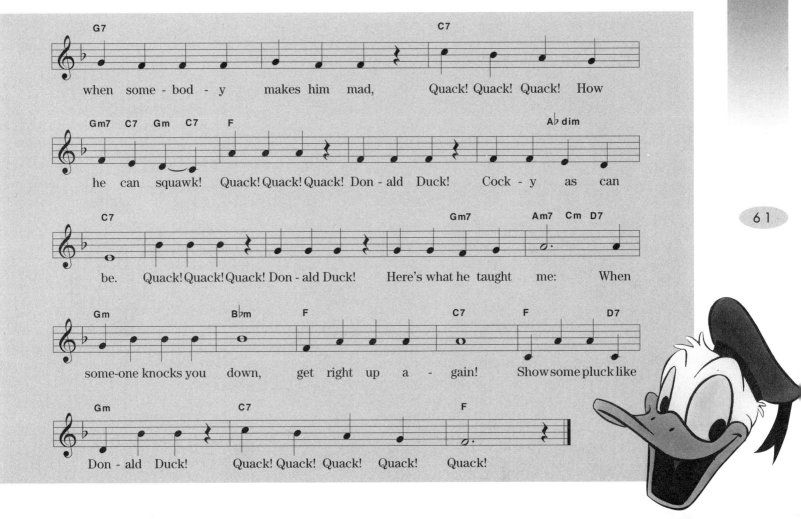

61

ZORRO (1957)

Out of the night when TV screens were bright, rode Walt Disney's "Zorro." This thrilling TV series was based on the stories of the Spanish-style Robin Hood written by Johnston McCulley. Set in Old California's Mission Era of the 1800s, "Zorro" related the exciting exploits of Don Diego de la Vega, the seemingly foppish aristocrat who by night was the dashing Zorro ("the Fox"). The caped outlaw used his sharp sword and especially his sharp wit to protect the poor and innocent from the cruel tyranny of a military dictator.

For the series' many action scenes, Walt Disney insisted on the realism of actual fencing foils, so it was essential that a Zorro be found with consummate fencing skill. After extensive auditioning, Guy Williams was cast; he was not only the perfect physical embodiment of the masked avenger, but he could wield a sword with the best of them. Williams' way with a guitar was a valuable asset, too; "Zorro" songs were penned by many composers, including such Disney stalwarts as Buddy Baker and Jimmie Dodd.

Disney sought a Spanish-flavored song to serve as a theme for his new TV hero. Composer George Bruns teamed with "Zorro" writer/director Norman Foster to create a stirring theme that included the trademark moment when Zorro boldly "carved a 'Z' with his blade"—the mark of Zorro.

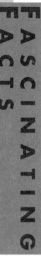

FASCINATING FACTS

- "Zorro" composer William Lava gave each character his own musical theme.
- Disney built an intricately detailed "Zorro City" on several acres of the Studio's backlot.
- Four different horses portrayed Zorro's steed; one specialized in rearing before the camera, as in the "Zorro" title sequence.
- Zorro creator Johnston McCulley was the series script supervisor.
- Guy Williams went on to star in another TV favorite, "Lost In Space."

TRIVIA TEASERS

1. Name Zorro's fiery black steed.
2. Don Diego's mute servant Bernardo (played by Gene Sheldon) had a secret that made him the perfect spy. What was it?
3. Name the bumbling officer played by Henry Calvin.
4. This Mouseketeer guest-starred on several "Zorro" episodes.
5. Besides his sword, what weapon did Zorro use to protect the innocent and punish the unjust?

ANSWERS 1. Tornado 2. He pretended to be deaf. 3. Sgt. Garcia 4. Annette Funicello 5. A whip

THEME FROM ZORRO

Words by
Norman Foster

Music by
George Bruns

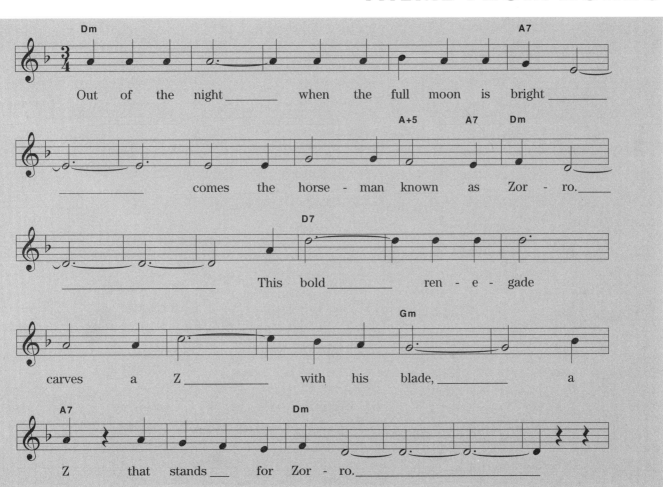

63

THEME FROM ZORRO (CONT'D.)

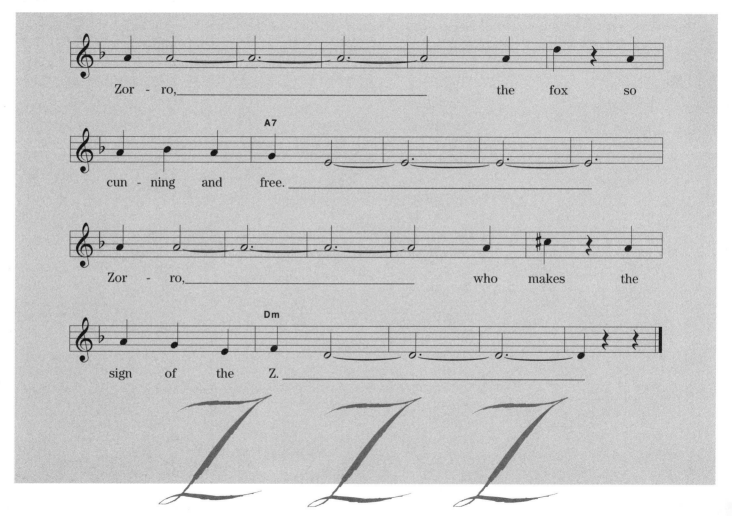

SLEEPING BEAUTY (1959)

Walt Disney envisioned *Sleeping Beauty* as his ultimate animated feature. To capture the rich pageantry of the original fairy tale about the beautiful princess who, under the spell of an evil curse, falls asleep after touching a spinning wheel's spindle, Disney decided to film the work in ultra-widescreen 70mm and assigned artist Eyvind Earle to design the production in a crisp, angular, opulent style that evoked 15th-century French illuminated manuscripts and medieval tapestries.

Disney's goal, according to sequence director Woolie Reitherman, was to match "visual perfection" with the eloquent music of Tchaikovsky's *Sleeping Beauty Ballet*. Staff composer George Bruns adapted the electrifying score for the film. "About one-third of the original ballet was preserved," noted Bruns, "and even in the adaptation the original flavor was never lost."

The love song "Once Upon a Dream" is the only *Sleeping Beauty* song not adapted by composer Bruns. Sammy Fain and Jack Lawrence did the honors for this romantic tune sung by Princess Aurora as she playfully dances with her animal friends. The solo becomes a duet when her dream lover, Prince Phillip, actually shows up.

Opera great Mary Costa provided the ethereally beautiful voice of Sleeping Beauty long before she achieved fame at the Met. "*Sleeping Beauty* is the thing I'm most proud of in my entire career," Costa has said. "It's a beautiful film to be associated with and I was thrilled to be able to do it."

TRIVIA TEASERS

1. What do the good fairies call Princess Aurora when they hide her in the woods?
2. With what special word do King Stefan and King Hubert toast the impending marriage of their children?
3. Name Prince Phillip's horse.
4. What are the names of the three good fairies?
5. What does the evil fairy Maleficent ultimately turn herself into to stop Prince Phillip from rescuing Aurora?

ANSWERS 1. Briar Rose 2. Skumps 3. Samson 4. Flora, Fauna, and Merryweather 5. A dragon

ONCE UPON A DREAM

Words & music
by Sammy Fain
& Jack Lawrence
Adapted from a
Theme by
Tchaikovsky

66

love me at once the way you did once up - on

a dream. _____

101 DALMATIANS (1961)

By 1961, Disney had done dogs—Bruno in *Cinderella*; *Lady and the Tramp*; and, of course, Mickey's pal, Pluto. But with his first feature of the 1960s, Disney went where no animation producer had dared to go by unleashing a film about not just one, but one hundred and one spotted dogs. A new photocopying process that transferred the pencil animation drawings directly to transparent cels not only made an animated movie about a hundred-plus Dalmatians possible, but also gave the film a distinctive pen-and-ink look that complements the sleek black-and-white elegance of the film's spotted stars.

The Disney artists also gave *One Hundred and One Dalmatians* a flat, modern look; the backgrounds were done in blocks of muted color, complete with black outlines to stylistically wed them to the animated characters.

The sophisticated styling perfectly suits the first Disney feature set in the contemporary world. A combination of comedy, drama, and espionage thriller, *One Hundred and One Dalmatians* centers on the doting Dalmatians, Pongo and Perdita, and their family of pups who are threatened by the demented and very determined Cruella De Vil and her diabolical dognapping scheme.

The Dalmatians' master, Roger Radcliff, is a songwriter, so it's ironic that *One Hundred and One Dalmatians* has only three songs, including the "Kanine Krunchies Commercial" jingle heard during the amusing cartoon sponsor break on the family TV, and "Dalmatian Plantation," composed by Roger in celebration of the bounty of bouncing spotted pups he adopts at film's end. Tunesmith Roger also pens "Cruella De Vil" in mock homage to the crafty Cruella herself. The saucy blues sound and wickedly clever lyrics perfectly capture Ms. De Vil's devilish personality.

69

TRIVIA TEASERS

1. Who provided the voice for Pongo?
2. What 1930s Disney cartoon is on the TV at the De Vil mansion?
3. What were the names of Cruella's nasty henchmen?
4. Who is the author of the original book on which *One Hundred and One Dalmatians* is based?
5. What does the canine community call its communication network, in which messages are conveyed via barking?

1. Rod Taylor 2. Springtime 3. Horace and Jasper Badun 4. Dodie Smith 5. The Twilight Bark
ANSWERS

CRUELLA DE VIL

**Words & Music
by Mel Leven**

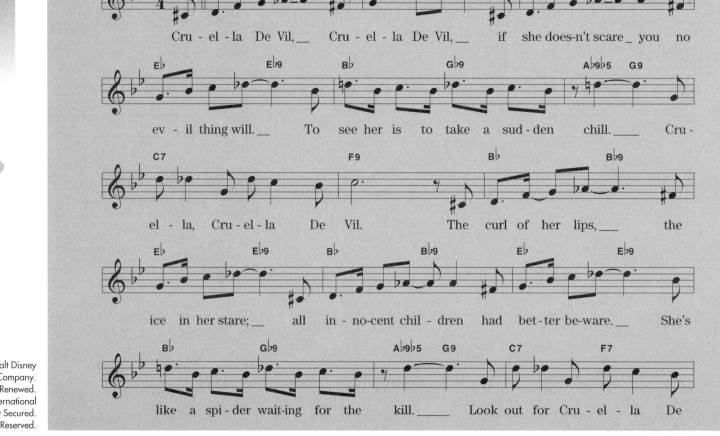

Cru - el - la De Vil, __ Cru - el - la De Vil, __ if she does-n't scare_ you no ev - il thing will. __ To see her is to take a sud - den chill. ___ Cru - el - la, Cru - el - la De Vil. The curl of her lips, ___ the ice in her stare; __ all in - no-cent chil - dren had bet-ter be-ware. __ She's like a spi - der wait-ing for the kill. ___ Look out for Cru - el - la De

til _____ Cru - el - la, Cru - el - la De Vil.

THE PARENT TRAP (1961)

"In my opinion," said Walt Disney, "Hayley Mills is the finest young talent to come along in at least 25 years." Plenty of people agreed with Disney; in *Pollyanna*, her Disney debut, Miss Mills earned glowing reviews and a special Academy Award as Outstanding Juvenile. So when it came to producing a follow-up film, Disney had to find a vehicle perfectly suited to the unique talents of his new star.

Disney discovered such a property in the unexpected form of a German novel, *Das Doppelte Löttchen* by Erich Kastner. Disney went to extraordinary lengths to secure screen rights to this story about identical twins, negotiating with two film companies and the German publisher in order to give young Hayley not one but two starring roles. *Pollyanna* writer/director David Swift adapted the German story into a hip American comedy about teenage twins who, separated as babies when their parents divorced, inadvertently meet at summer camp. Initially enemies, the girls team up and switch places in a plot to reunite their parents (Maureen O'Hara and Brian Keith).

Walt Disney wanted rock music to match the sharp wit of the script: He called on the talents of Richard M. and Robert B. Sherman, a pair of brother songwriters who had written a series of rock 'n' roll hits for Annette Funicello. The project went through a number of titles, including *We Belong Together* and *Petticoats and Bluejeans*, and the Shermans wrote songs to fit each new title. One of these tunes the Shermans altered into a rocking duet for Hayley to sing with herself. Mills' performance of "Let's Get Together" shows off the moviemaking magic that made it possible for the young actress to play opposite herself. Hayley's recording of "Let's Get Together" became a top seller, reaching Number 1 on the charts in England. Walt Disney himself titled the film *The Parent Trap* and it became one of his biggest hits of the 1960s.

73

FASCINATING FACTS

- Walt Disney cast Hayley Mills in *Pollyanna* after seeing her in *Tiger Bay*, a British film Disney screened to see her father, Sir John Mills, whom he cast as the father in *Swiss Family Robinson* (1960).
- *The Parent Trap* writer/director David Swift was a Disney animator in the 1930s and early 40s.
- Before *The Parent Trap*, *Das Doppelte Löttchen* was made into a German film and a British film.
- *The Parent Trap* was the first of seven theatrical films Brian Keith made for the Disney Studio.

TRIVIA TEASERS

1. What are the twins' names?
2. What is the name of the summer camp attended by the girls?
3. Who sang *The Parent Trap*'s title song under the opening credits?
4. Name the four other Disney theatrical films Hayley Mills starred in after *Pollyanna* and *The Parent Trap*.
5. Who plays the twins' maternal grandfather?

ANSWERS 1. *Susan and Sharon* 2. *Camp Inch* 3. *Annette Funicello and Tommy Sands* 4. *In Search of the Castaways* (1962), *Summer Magic* (1963), *The Moon-Spinners* (1964), *That Darn Cat!* (1965) 5. *Charlie Ruggles*

LET'S GET TOGETHER

Words & music
by Richard M.
Sherman &
Robert B.
Sherman

74

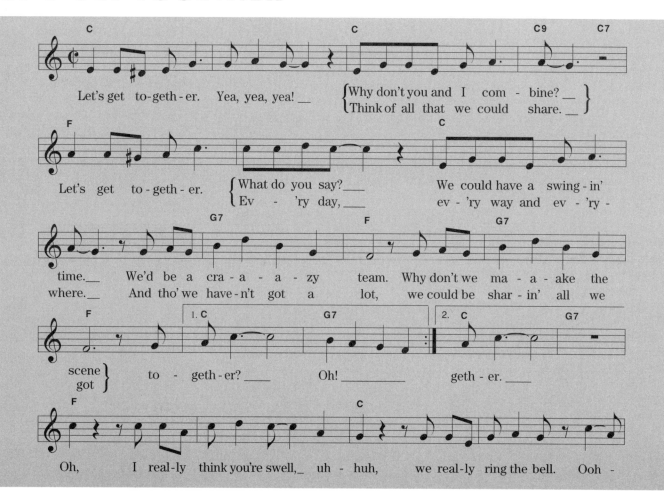

Let's get to-geth-er. Yea, yea, yea! __
{ Why don't you and I com- bine? __ }
{ Think of all that we could share. __ }

Let's get to-geth-er.
{ What do you say? ___
{ Ev- 'ry day, ___
We could have a swing-in'
ev-'ry way and ev-'ry-

time. __ We'd be a cra-a-a-zy team. Why don't we ma-a-ake the
where. __ And tho' we have-n't got a lot, we could be shar-in' all we

scene } to- geth-er? ____ Oh! _____ geth- er. ____
got }

Oh, I real-ly think you're swell,_ uh-huh, we real-ly ring the bell. Ooh-

NEW YORK WORLD'S FAIR (1964-1965)

For the spectacular 1964 International Exposition in New York City, Disney "imagineered" four innovative exhibitions. Walt planned the four Disney-designed shows—Great Moments with Mr. Lincoln, Magic Skyway, It's a Small World, and Carousel of Progress—to showcase the newly-invented Audio-Animatronics technology. This "space-age electronic" technology gave voice and motion to three-dimensional figures. Audio-Animatronics would figure prominently in Disney's future plans, and he saw the World's Fair as a means of experimenting with this new medium.

But Disney's priority was, as always, entertainment. For the four-act, six-theatre revolving Carousel of Progress and its depiction of the evolution of the American household from 1890 to the future, Walt sought a theme that would celebrate the achievements of the past and the optimistic excitement of the future. Those ever-reliable songwriting Sherman brothers delivered with "There's a Great Big Beautiful Tomorrow." Walt so enjoyed the Carousel of Progress theme song that he sang the tune with the Shermans in a special film for General Electric, sponsor of the exhibit. "Sounds pretty good," Walt said after finishing the song. "In fact, that's just the right spirit."

It's a Small World was created for Pepsi-Cola and UNICEF, the United Nations children's fund. For this musical fantasy featuring the charming Audio-Animatronics figures of children from over one-hundred lands, Walt really challenged his brotherly tunesmiths. Walt's tall order: "a song that is universal, that can be sung in any language, with any type of instrumentation, simultaneously." The Shermans more than met the challenge: "It's a Small World" is a simple ditty that has become one of the most well-known, most-performed, and best-loved songs in the Disney canon.

When It's a Small World moved to Disneyland Park at the close of the World's Fair, it was cause for celebration: Colorfully costumed in their native garb, children from all over the world joined Walt Disney in the dedication ceremonies as "the happiest cruise that ever sailed" found its rightful home at "the happiest place on earth."

TRIVIA TEASERS

1. These mammoth Audio-Animatronics beasts were transplanted from the World's Fair's Magic Skyway to the Disneyland Primeval World.
2. Name the only major country not represented in It's a Small World at Disneyland Park.
3. This country performer, who narrated many of Disney's TV nature stories, was the lead vocalist on "There's a Great Big Beautiful Tomorrow."
4. In what year did It's a Small World debut at Disneyland?

ANSWERS 1. Dinosaurs 2. The United States 3. Rex Allen 4. 1966

IT'S A SMALL WORLD

Words & music
by Richard M.
Sherman &
Robert B.
Sherman

77

IT'S A SMALL WORLD (CONT'D.)

small world, af - ter all. It's a small, small world.

Additional Lyrics:
There is just one moon and one golden sun
And a smile means friendship to ev'ryone,
Though the mountains divide
And the oceans are wide,
It's a small world after all.

THERE'S A GREAT BIG BEAUTIFUL TOMORROW

Words & music
by Richard M.
Sherman &
Robert B.
Sherman

There's a great, big, beau-ti-ful to-mor-row___

shin-ing at the end of ev-'ry day.___ There's a great, big,

beau-ti-ful to-mor-row___ and to-mor-row's just a dream a-

way.___ Man has a dream and that's the start; he

fol-lows his dream with mind and heart. And when it be-

MARY POPPINS (1964)

A bottomless carpetbag of magical delights, *Mary Poppins* showcases the entertainment elements Walt Disney loved: animation, live action, special effects, Audio-Animatronics figures, and, of course, music. Walt envisioned the story of a nanny who flies in on the East Wind to touch the lives of young Jane and Michael Banks with magic as a full-fledged musical. He assigned the prolific Sherman brothers to the project and they wrote 14 winning songs.

To musically establish the character of the wondrous nanny, the Shermans composed a keynote song for Mary Poppins. But when Julie Andrews was cast in the lead role and heard the sentimental ballad, she felt Mary Poppins would sing a snappier, less direct song. Inspiration came to the brothers in the form of Robert Sherman's son, who had received a vaccination on a sugar cube. Both brothers agreed, "That's Mary Poppins!" "A Spoonful of Sugar" to help the medicine go down was born.

The Shermans were moved to write the upbeat yet haunting Academy Award winner "Chim Chim Cher-ee" by a story sketch of a chimney sweep drawn by Bill Walsh's co-screenwriter Don DaGradi. "It was just so picturesque and touching," recalled Richard Sherman, "we knew that was a song. There's a beautiful English legend about shaking hands with a sweep being good luck, and we loved that concept."

"Supercalifragilisticexpialidocious" is the ultimate specially-coined-Disney-word song. "We took a nonsense word we had as kids in summer camp and added a few more syllables," explained Robert Sherman. The tongue-twisting word was a talisman for Jane and Michael to bring back from the cartoon fantasy world. "As kids, our word was one we had that no adult had," pointed out Richard Sherman. "It was our special word, and we wanted the Banks children to have the same feeling."

TRIVIA TEASERS

1. What is the street address of the Banks family's London home?
2. What "reverse-lullaby" does Mary Poppins sing when the children refuse to go to sleep?
3. Who sells bread crumbs on the steps of St. Paul's Cathedral? What actress portrays her?
4. What sort of umbrella does Mary Poppins carry?
5. What cause prevents Mrs. Banks from being at home much of the time?

ANSWERS 1. 17 Cherry Tree Lane 2. "Stay Awake" 3. The Bird Woman; Jane Darwell 4. A parrot-headed umbrella 5. The Suffragette Movement

A SPOONFUL OF SUGAR

Words & music
by Richard M.
Sherman &
Robert B.
Sherman

In ev-'ry job that must be done there is an el-e-ment of fun. You find the fun and, snap, the job's a game. And ev-'ry task you un-der-take be-comes a piece of cake. A lark! A spree! It's ver-y clear to see that a spoon-ful of sug-ar helps the med-i-cine go down, the

8 3

A SPOONFUL OF SUGAR (CONT'D.)

Additional Lyrics:

2. A robin feathering his nest
   Has very little time to rest
   While gathering his bits of twine and twig.
   Though quite intent in his pursuit,
   He has a merry tune to toot.
   He knows a song will move the job along. For a...
   refrain

3. The honey bees that fetch the nectar
   From the flowers to the comb
   Never tire of ever buzzing to and fro,
   Because they take a little nip
   From ev'ry flower that they sip.
   And hence, they find their task is not a grind. For a...
   refrain

SUPERCALIFRAGILISTICEXPIALIDOCIOUS

Words & music
by Richard M.
Sherman &
Robert B.
Sherman

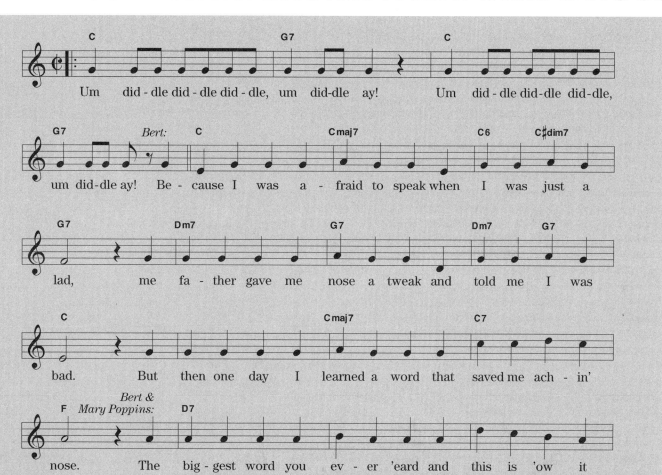

85

Additional Lyrics:

Mary Poppins: He traveled all around the world
And ev'rywhere he went,
He'd use his word and all would say,
"There goes a clever gent!"

Bert: When dukes and ma'arajas
Pass the time of day with me,
I say me special word
And then they ask me out to tea.

All: Oh! Supercalifragilisticexpialidocious!
Even though the sound of it
Is something quite atrocious,
If you say it loud enough,
You'll always sound precocious.
Supercalifragilisticexpialidocious!

Mary Poppins: So when the cat has got your tongue,
There's no need to dismay,
Just summon up this word
And then you've got a lot to say.

Bert: But better use it carefully
Or it can change your life.

Pearlie: One night I said it to me girl
And now me girl's me wife.

All: She's supercalifragilisticexpialidocious!
Supercalifragilisticexpialidocious!
Supercalifragilisticexpialidocious!
Supercalifragilisticexpialidocious!

CHIM CHIM CHER-EE

Words & music
by Richard M.
Sherman &
Robert B.
Sherman

88

Chim chim - in - ey, chim chim - in - ey, chim chim cher - ee! A
sweep is as luck - y as luck - y can be.
Chim chim - in - ey, chim chim - in - ey, chim chim cher - oo! Good
luck will rub off when I shakes 'ands with you. Or
blow me a kiss, and that's luck - y, too.

Additional Lyrics:

Now, as the ladder of life 'as been strung,
You may think a sweep's on the bottom-most rung.
Though I spends me time in the ashes and smoke,
In this 'ole wide world there's no 'appier bloke.

I choose me bristles with pride, yes, I do:
A broom for the shaft and a brush for the flue.
Though I'm covered with soot from me 'ead to me toes,
A sweep knows 'e's welcome wherever 'e goes.

Up where the smoke is all billered and curled,
'Tween pavement and stars, is the chimney sweep world.
When there's 'ardly no day nor 'ardly no night,
There's things 'alf in shadow and 'alfway in light.
On the rooftops of London, coo, what a sight!

Chim chiminey, chim chiminey, chim chim cher-ee!
When you're with a sweep, you're in glad company.
Nowhere is there a more 'appier crew
Than them wot sings, "Chim chim cher-ee, chim cher-oo!"
Chim chiminey, chim chim cher-ee, chim cher-oo!

WINNIE THE POOH (1966)

Walt Disney discovered the Winnie the Pooh books through his daughter Diane. "Dad would hear me laughing alone in my room and come in to see what I was laughing at," Diane Disney Miller remembered. "It was usually the gentle, whimsical humor of A.A. Milne's Pooh stories." When Disney decided to adapt Christopher Robin's huggable, honey-loving bear for animation, he wanted the charm and whimsy of Milne's writing to arrive on the screen intact. The Sherman brothers were assigned to set the stories to song. But "when Walt asked us to read *Winnie the Pooh*," said Richard Sherman, "we couldn't get with the subject right away. One day during the filming of *Mary Poppins*, we asked Julie Andrews' then-husband, Tony Walton, about Pooh, since he was raised in England. He spent several hours with us explaining how important the Pooh stories were to him while he was growing up. He had identified with pudgy Pooh, who always came out on top.

"It was like a door opening up. All of a sudden we understood how to read the stories, and we reread them and got this kind of joyous abandon. We could go into that Hundred-Acre Wood and be those characters...and then the songs just started flowing out of us."

The beguiling, lullaby-like "Winnie the Pooh," the first Pooh song the Shermans wrote, charmingly introduces all the residents of Christopher Robin's "enchanted neighborhood"—especially the "willy-nilly, silly ole bear" at the heart of it all.

Winnie the Pooh and the Honey Tree (1966) was a solid hit and another Pooh short was put into production. This new featurette added the outrageously rambunctious Tigger to the cast. For this egotistical tiger, convinced that "he's the only one," the Shermans created a suitably bouncy tune extolling the wonderfulness of being a Tigger. "The Wonderful Thing About Tiggers" set up the one-of-a-kind critter as a springy, striped star and helped *Winnie the Pooh and the Blustery Day* (1968) win an Academy Award as Best Cartoon Short Subject.

TRIVIA TEASERS

1. This famous ventriloquist is the "bouncy" voice of Tigger.
2. What name does Pooh "live under"?
3. Pooh is afraid these creatures will steal his honey.
4. What is the name of Piglet's grandfather?
5. Pooh uses this to help him float through the air like a "little black rain cloud."
6. Which Pooh character is "not in the book, ya know!"

ANSWERS 1. *Paul Winchell* 2. *Mr. Sanders* 3. *Heffalumps and woozles* 4. *Trespassers Will* 5. *A balloon* 6. *Gopher*

WINNIE THE POOH

Words & music by Richard M. Sherman & Robert B. Sherman

WINNIE THE POOH (CONT'D.)

Pooh!   Win - nie the Pooh,   Win - nie the Pooh,   tub-by lit-tle cub-by all

stuffed with fluff. He's Win - nie the Pooh,   Win - nie the Pooh,   wil - ly nil - ly sil - ly ole

bear.

THE WONDERFUL THING ABOUT TIGGERS

Words & music by Richard M. Sherman & Robert B. Sherman

1., 3. The won-der-ful thing a-bout tig-gers ____ is tig-gers are won-der-ful
2. won-der-ful thing a-bout tig-gers ____ is tig-gers are won-der-ful

things! Their tops are made out of rub-ber; ___ their bot-toms are made out of
chaps! They're load-ed with vim and with vig-or; ___ they love to leap in your

springs! They're boun-cy, troun-cy, floun-cy, poun-cy,} Fun! Fun! Fun! Fun! Fun!
laps! They're jump-y, bump-y, clump-y, thump-y, }

But the most won-der-ful thing a-bout tig-gers is I'm the on-ly

one! Oh, the one! Tig-gers are cud-di-ly

93

THE WONDERFUL THING ABOUT TIGGERS (CONT'D.)

fel - las. _____ Tig-gers are aw - ful - ly sweet. Ev - 'ry - one el - es is

jeal - ous. _____ That's why I re - peat and re - peat: The

THE JUNGLE BOOK (1967)

The jungle's jumpin' in Walt Disney's adaptation of Rudyard Kipling's *The Jungle Book*, a swinging safari of comedy and colorful characters. And the unofficial king of this jungle is Baloo, the happy-go-lucky bear, who befriends the man-cub, Mowgli.

But at first the animators and story artists found the big bear a challenge. A variety of voices was tested in an attempt to give a new personality to Baloo, who was a gruff teacher of jungle law in the Kipling original. "We'd gone through a whole lot of guys," recalled director Woolie Reitherman. "Finally Walt came back from a party in Palm Springs, and Phil Harris had been there. He said, 'Why don't you try Phil Harris?' 'Gee,' some of the animators said, 'Phil Harris in a Rudyard Kipling film?' Walt said, 'Why not?'"

The jazzy lingo of gravel-voiced bandleader Harris inspired the artists and brought the bear to bouncy life; Harris's facial expressions and with-the-beat body language all became part of the bear's carefree performance. When story artist Bill Peet suggested a theme song for Baloo called "The Bare Necessities," Terry Gilkyson, who had written songs for several Disney films, took that concept and ran with it.

Animator Ollie Johnston had no trouble animating Baloo singing his theme song once he saw Walt Disney act out how Phil Harris—and therefore Baloo—always moved to a beat. The upbeat syncopation of "The Bare Necessities" set the mood and tempo for this all-important sequence that established the relationship between boy and bear.

Originally conceived as a bit player, Baloo became *The Jungle Book*'s star, creating memorable movie moments, whether as a caring father-figure to Mowgli, or as an energetic song and dance partner singing "I Wan'na Be Like You" in drag (jungle-style) with King Louie.

Phil Harris has commented that his performance as Baloo has made him immortal.

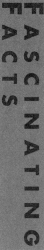

TRIVIA TEASERS

1. What human "secret" did King Louie want?
2. Mowgli was raised from infancy by what sort of animal?
3. Who was the voice of the sophisticated tiger Shere Khan?
4. What is the name of Mowgli's very proper panther protector?
5. What kind of animal is Kaa?

ANSWERS 1. Fire 2. Wolves 3. George Sanders 4. Bagheera 5. A python

THE BARE NECESSITIES

Words & music
by Terry Gilkyson

96

I WAN'NA BE LIKE YOU (THE MONKEY SONG)

Words & music
by Richard M.
Sherman &
Robert B.
Sherman

98

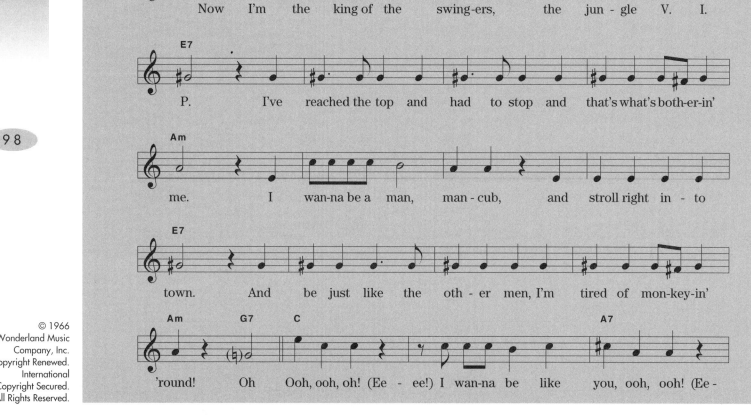

Now I'm the king of the swing-ers, the jun - gle V. I. P. I've reached the top and had to stop and that's what's both-er-in' me. I wan-na be a man, man - cub, and stroll right in - to town. And be just like the oth - er men, I'm tired of mon-key-in' 'round! Oh Ooh, ooh, oh! (Ee - ee!) I wan-na be like you, ooh, ooh! (Ee -

THE LITTLE MERMAID (1989)

A high water mark in animation, *The Little Mermaid* was the first Disney fairy tale since *Sleeping Beauty* (1959). Walt Disney himself had explored making a feature version of Hans Christian Andersen's *The Little Mermaid* in the 1940s, so it was the fulfillment of a Disney destiny when the "new generation" of animation artists produced the story of Ariel, the misunderstood mermaid who longs to be part of the human world.

As with many of Disney's animated classics, *The Little Mermaid*'s music is integral to the storytelling. Seven new tunes were used to both advance and enhance the story as a result of the animation team's close collaboration with the songwriting team of Howard Ashman and Alan Menken, famed for their off-beat, off-Broadway musical *Little Shop of Horrors*. A lifelong fan of Andersen's works, Howard Ashman eagerly accepted the assignment of transforming the famous fairy tale into a musical.

The process harkened back to Disney's Golden Age. "Then," observed Menken, "the music was written before they began animating. In many ways we've gone back to that tradition for this film by laying the songs out early in the storyboarding process. There are a lot of places where they've animated right to the music. It's amazing to see the way the animators bring life to the music by causing something inanimate to act. It's like having the greatest actors in the world performing your material."

"Coming from a musical theater background," elaborated Ashman, "we're used to writing songs for characters in situations. For *The Little Mermaid* we wanted songs that would really move the story forward and keep things driving ahead. Instead of stopping to sing a song, it's more like you get to a certain point where the crab has to convince the mermaid not to go up above the water and change her life, so he sings 'Under the Sea.'"

"Under the Sea," Sebastian's salute to undersea living, won an Oscar as Best Song; the entire score also received an Academy Award, making *The Little Mermaid* the most honored Disney film score since *Mary Poppins*.

100

TRIVIA TEASERS

1. What's the name of Ariel's finny little fish friend?
2. What stage and TV favorite supplies the voice for Ursula the Sea Witch?
3. What royal command does Ariel break by rescuing Prince Eric?
4. What sort of "treasure" does Ariel keep in her secret grotto?
5. Ariel gives this to Ursula in return for a pair of legs.

ANSWERS 1. *Flounder* 2. *Pat Carroll* 3. *Merpeople are forbidden to have contact with humans.* 4. *Human artifacts and belongings* 5. *Her voice*

UNDER THE SEA

Lyrics by
Howard Ashman

Music by
Alan Menken

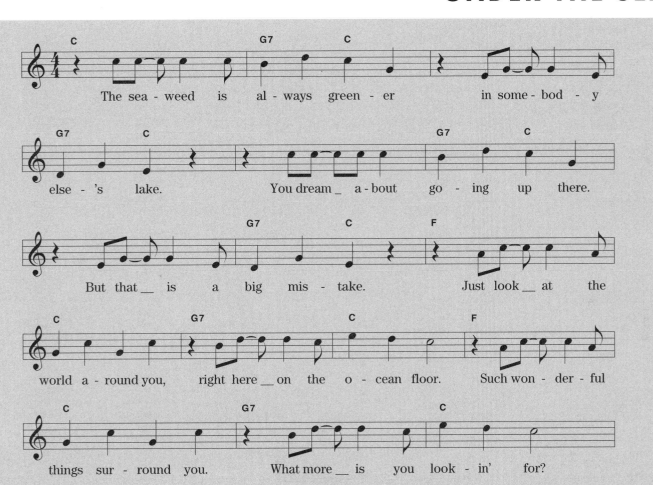

101

Additional Lyrics:

Down here all the fish is happy
As off through the waves they roll.
The fish on the land ain't happy.
They sad 'cause they in the bowl.
But fish in the bowl is lucky, they in for a worser fate.
One day when the boss get hungry
Guess who gon' be on the plate.
Under the sea, under the sea.
Nobody beat us, fry us, and eat us in fricassee.
We what the land folks loves to cook.
Under the sea we off the hook.
We got no troubles. Life is the bubbles under the sea.
Under the sea.
Since life is sweet here we got the beat here naturally.
Even the sturgeon an' the ray,
They get the urge 'n' start to play.
We got the spirit, you got to hear it under the sea.
The newt play the lute.
The carp play the harp.
The plaice play the bass.

And they soundin' sharp.
The bass play the brass.
The chub play the tub.
The fluke is the duke of soul.
The ray he can play.
The ling's on the strings.
The trout rockin' out.
The blackfish, she sings.
The smelt and the sprat, they know where it's at.
An' oh, that blowfish blow.
Under the sea. Under the sea.
When the sardine begin the beguine it's music to me.
What do they got, a lot of sand?
We got a hot crustacean band.
Each little clam here know how to jam here
Under the sea.
Each little slug here cuttin' a rug here under the sea.
Each little snail here know how to wail here.
That's why it's hotter under the water.
Ya we in luck here down in the muck here
Under the sea.

BEAUTY AND THE BEAST (1991)

Disney's 30th full-length animated feature, *Beauty and the Beast*, retells the classic "tale as old as time" through the art of animation, enhanced with the sophisticated lyrics and memorable melodies of Howard Ashman and Alan Menken. Walt Disney gave serious consideration to transforming the beloved fairy tale into an animated feature, but it wasn't until four decades later that the Disney animation staff took on the challenge. Howard Ashman was instrumental in developing narrative ideas, including the breakthrough concept of turning the objects in the Beast's enchanted castle into individual personalities.

Their moment in the spotlight is the spectacular Busby Berkeley-style production number, "Be Our Guest." "This song was written basically to fill a situation in a story," said Alan Menken of the French music hall-style song performed by Lumiere the romantic candelabra, Mrs. Potts the warmhearted teapot, and Cogsworth the wound-up clock. "Our heads were filled with all the wonderful images that could be provided by the animators, and as usual they exceeded our expectations."

"Gaston," described by Menken as a "barroom waltz," sets up the character of Belle's determined suitor as a fairy tale-style male chauvinist egotist.

The title song, a combination ballad/lullaby, is the film's emotionally powerful turning point. "I think simplicity is the key to that particular song," mused Menken. "We wanted it to be gentler and smaller as opposed to some ballads that are large and heroic in scope."

Beauty and the Beast is the first motion picture to ever have three of its songs ("Belle," "Be Our Guest," and "Beauty and the Beast") nominated for an Academy Award. "Beauty and the Beast" received the Oscar and Menken's musical score also won as Best Score. More significantly, *Beauty and the Beast* made history as the first animated feature to be nominated as Best Picture.

104

GASTON

Lyrics by
Howard Ashman

Music by
Alan Menken

105

No one's slick as Gas - ton. No one's quick as Gas - ton. No one's neck's as in - cred - i - bly thick as Gas - ton! For there's no man in town half as man - ly. Per - fect! A pure par - a - gon! _____ You can ask an - y Tom, Dick, or Stan - ley and they'll

GASTON (CONT'D.)

tell you whose team they pre - fer to be on! *Chorus:* No -

one's been like Gas - ton, a king - pin like Gas - ton. No one's

got a swell cleft in his chin like Gas - ton! As a

spe - ci - men, yes, I'm in - tim - i - dat - ing!

Chorus: My, what a guy, that Gas - ton!

BE OUR GUEST

Lyrics by
Howard Ashman

Music by
Alan Menken

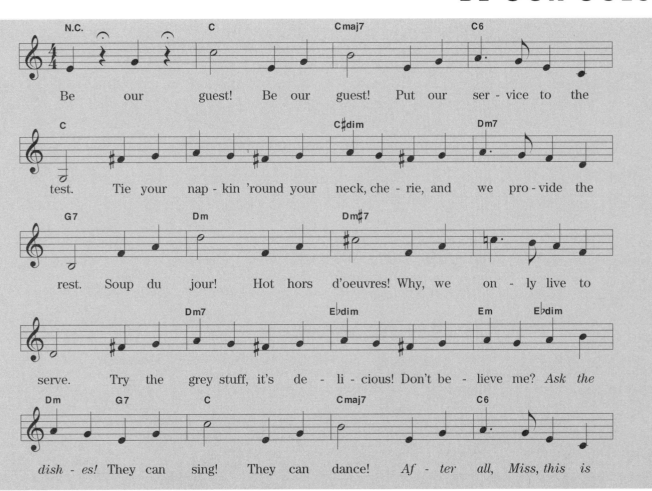

BE OUR GUEST (CONT'D.)

France! And a din - ner here is nev - er sec - ond

best. Go on, un - fold your men - u, take a

glance, and then _____ you'll be our

guest, *oui,* our guest! Be our

guest!

Additional Lyrics:

Lumiere:
Beef ragout!
Cheese souffle!
Pie and pudding "en flambe!"
We'll prepare and serve with flair
A culinary cabaret!
You're alone and you're scared,
But the banquet's all prepared.
No one's gloomy or complaining
While the flatware's entertaining.
We tell jokes.
I do tricks with my fellow candlesticks.

Mugs:
And it's all in perfect taste.
That you can bet!

All:
Come on and lift your glass.
You've won your own free pass
To be our guest!
Be our guest!
Be our guest!

Mrs Potts:
It's a guest!
It's a guest!
Sakes alive,
Well, I'll be blessed!
Wine's been poured and thank the Lord
I've had the napkins freshly pressed.
With dessert she'll want tea.
And my dear, that's fine with me.
While the cups do their soft shoeing,
I'll be bubbling!
I'll be brewing!
I'll get warm, piping hot!

Heaven's sakes!
Is that a spot?
Clean it up!
We want the company impressed!
We've got a lot to do.
Is it one lump or two
For you, our guest?

Chorus:
She's our guest!

Mrs. Potts:
She's our guest!

Chorus:
Be our guest!
Be our guest!
Our command is your request.
It's ten years since we had anybody here,
And we're obsessed.
With your meal,
With your ease,
Yes, indeed,
We aim to please.
While the candlelight's still glowing
Let us help you,
We'll keep going.
Course by course,
One by one!
'Til you shout,
"Enough. I'm done!"
Then we'll sing you off to sleep as you digest.
Tonight you'll prop your feet up!
But for now, let's eat up!
Be our guest!
Be our guest!
Be our guest!

BEAUTY AND THE BEAST

**Lyrics by
Howard Ashman**

**Music by
Alan Menken**

Tale as old as time, true as it can be. Bare-ly e-ven friends, then some-bod-y bends un-ex-pect-ed - ly. Just a lit-tle change. Small, to say the least. Both a lit - tle scared, nei-ther one pre-pared. Beau-ty and the Beast. Ev - er just the same. Ev - er a sur-prise. Ev - er as be - fore, ev - er just as

ALADDIN (1992)

Aladdin, the ancient legend of a lad and his magical lamp, was seen in a new light in Disney's new-wave animated musical. A magic carpet ride of action-adventure, outlandish comedy, and bold, vibrant visuals, *Aladdin* was conceived from the start as a story-told-through-song by lyricist Howard Ashman.

"Howard wrote a treatment which was different from the story that has been animated now," said Menken, "and we wrote the songs to fit that treatment. Three of them remain—'Friend Like Me,' 'Arabian Nights,' and 'Prince Ali'—but you start from the story, you start from the characters and where the plot goes...and you find your place for the songs."

Setting a properly mysterious and exotic mood for the tale about to unfold, "Arabian Nights" opens the movie with an "orthodox Arabic/Middle Eastern" tone. "We wanted to incorporate Arabian music into this Arabian tale," explained Menken.

Already a tasty dish, the *Aladdin* project was further spiced up by the directing/writing team of John Musker and Ron Clements, who ladled in heaping helpings of romance, adventure, and comedy—and this new recipe called for some new songs. Menken teamed up with lyricist Tim Rice, former collaborator with Andrew Lloyd Webber, for some additional tunes to meet the growing demands of the story. Together, they composed "One Jump Ahead," establishing Aladdin's "diamond-in-the-rough" character from his first "jump" on screen. For both Aladdin and his true love, Princess Jasmine, the newly teamed duo composed "A Whole New World," a sweeping ballad sung on a starry Arabian night during an around-the-world magic carpet flight. "I really came to a new place with this song," Menken reveals. "It's among the broadest and most romantic songs I've ever written." "A Whole New World" was awarded an Oscar as Best Song and the music Menken created to underscore the magical movie won the Academy Award for Best Score, affirming *Aladdin*'s status as a new classic.

112

ARABIAN NIGHTS

Lyrics by
Howard Ashman

Music by
Alan Menken

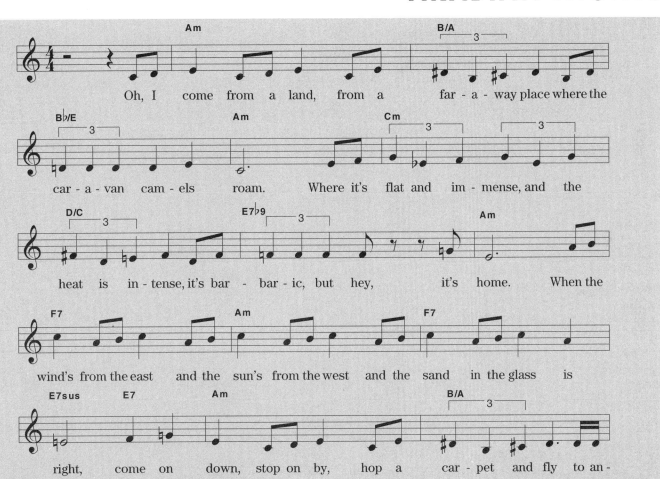

113

ARABIAN NIGHTS (CONT'D.)

oth - er A - ra - bi - an night. A - ra - bi - an nights, _____

__ like A - ra - bi - an days, more of - ten than not are hot - ter than

hot in a lot - ta good ways. A - ra - bi - an nights, _____

__ 'neath A - ra - bi - an moons, a fool off his guard could fall and fall

hard out there on the dunes.

A WHOLE NEW WORLD

Music by
Alan Menken

Lyrics by
Tim Rice

115

A WHOLE NEW WORLD (CONT'D.)

view. No-one to tell us no or where to go or

Jasmine:

say we're on - ly dream - ing. A whole new world, a daz - zling

place I nev - er knew. But when I'm way up here, it's

crys - tal clear that now I'm in a

whole new world with you.

THE LION KING (1994)

For *The Lion King*, the Disney animation crew developed the completely original story of Simba, a lion prince who grows from a carefree cub into a responsible adult who can accept his rightful place as "king of the beasts."

Music is the pride of *The Lion King*, and the movie's creators brought together some king-sized talent to set the stunning visuals and compelling story to song. Lyricist Tim Rice invited composer and pop performer Elton John to join him in creating *The Lion King*'s music. "I jumped at the chance because I knew Disney was a class act, and I liked the storyline and the people immediately," revealed John. "For me, this project was exciting and challenging because I had to write differently from what I could write for myself. I was pleased that the story was about animals because *The Jungle Book* is one of my favorite Disney films."

In working with Elton John, Tim Rice reversed his usual lyrical process. "Up until now, about 95% of the lyrics I've written have been done to a tune," explained Rice. "Elton is one of those rare examples of a composer who actually likes to get the words first. In the case of a film like *The Lion King*, that proved to be quite useful because the key thing with a Disney animated feature is to get the story line dead right. Everything flows from the story."

The most challenging *Lion King* song was "Can You Feel the Love Tonight." The first to be written and the last to be perfected, the ballad saw many changes as the story evolved; Rice wrote 15 sets of lyrics for the song over several years. At one point, the song was to be sung by the warthog/ meerkat comedy team, Pumbaa and Timon, but John felt strongly about the role of a love song in a Disney film and convinced the directors to have the song reflect Simba's and Nala's awakening love.

The last song composed was "Hakuna Matata," a delightfully carefree, zydeco-flavored tune sung by Broadway stars Nathan Lane and Ernie Sabella to express Pumbaa's and Timon's kick-back take on life.

117

TRIVIA TEASERS

1. Name King Mufasa's fussy but loyal secretary bird.
2. This young star of TV's "Home Improvement" is the voice of young Simba.
3. Where does the Lion King hold court over his domain?
4. What relation is the evil Scar to little Simba?
5. Which laughing hyena laughs the most?

ANSWERS 1. Zazu 2. Jonathan Taylor Thomas 3. Pride Rock 4. Uncle 5. Ed

HAKUNA MATATA

Music by
Elton John

Lyrics by
Tim Rice

118

Ha - ku - na ma - ta - ta... _____ what a won - der - ful

phrase. Ha - ku - na ma - ta - ta... _____

ain't no pass - ing craze. It means no wor - ries

for the rest of your days. _____ It's our prob - lem - free _____ phi -

los - o - phy. _____ Ha - ku - na ma - ta - ta. _____

CAN YOU FEEL THE LOVE TONIGHT

Music by
Elton John

Lyrics by
Tim Rice

It's e-nough for this wide - eyed wan-der-er____

that we got this far.__ And can you feel__ the love__ to-night,__

how it's laid to rest?_____ It's e-nough to make

kings and vag - a - bonds__ be -

lieve the ver - y best.

120

POCAHONTAS (1995)

The pristine beauty of the American wilderness and the dignity of the human spirit form the compelling backdrop of *Pocahontas*, Disney's 33rd full-length animated feature. *Pocahontas* continues the Disney tradition of tuneful storytelling with seven songs that are integral to this romanticized tale of the Powhatan Indian heroine and her encounter with the ways of the white man's world in the form of Captain John Smith and the English settlers led by Governor Ratcliffe.

Disney veteran Alan Menken teamed up with Broadway lyricist Stephen Schwartz to create an integrated song score which gives musical voice to many of *Pocahontas*'s dramatic and emotional high points. "Steady as the Beating Drum" expresses the regularity and harmony of the Native Americans' way of life and the affinity they feel for the natural world that surrounds them, whereas "Just Around the River-bend" reveals Pocahontas's adventurous spirit and her dreams for the future.

"Colors of the Wind" is the beautiful heroine's musical lesson to Smith on the Native Americans' respect and appreciation for the world around them.

Indeed the natural world takes on a life of its own in the film, from the guidance and comfort Pocahontas receives from Grandmother Willow, to the spiritual aspect of the blowing wind.

Weaving historical fact together with legend and fantasy, *Pocahontas* is unique among Disney animated features in its emphasis on real human characters and its moving dramatic tone.

FASCINATING FACTS

- Pocahontas's speaking voice is provided by Native American actress Irene Bedard, who also appeared in Walt Disney Pictures' live-action adventure, *Squanto, A Warrior's Tale* (1994).
- *Pocahontas* is the first Disney animated feature to be inspired by a real-life figure.
- Animator Glen Keane drew his first concept sketch of Pocahontas on an animation drawing of Aladdin.

TRIVIA TEASERS

1. What is the name of Pocahontas's mischievous raccoon pal?
2. What is the name of the ship that brought the English settlers to the New World?
3. Where and when is *Pocahontas* set?
4. What gesture of friendship does the departing John Smith receive from Powhatan?

ANSWERS
1. Meeko 2. The Susan Constant 3. In the area we now call Virginia, in 1607 4. The chief gives him his ceremonial robe.

COLORS OF THE WIND

Music by
Alan Menken

Lyrics by
Stephen Schwartz

land on;   the earth is   just   a   dead thing you   can   claim;   but

I know ev - 'ry rock and tree and   crea-ture   has   a   life,   has   a   spir - it, has a

name.   You   think the on - ly   peo - ple who are   peo - ple   are   the

peo - ple   who look and think like   you,   but   if   you walk the foot-steps of   a

strang - er   you'll learn things you nev - er   knew you nev - er   knew.___ Have you

COLORS OF THE WIND (CONT'D.)

ev - er heard the wolf cry to the blue corn moon, or

asked the grin-ning bob-cat why he grinned? Can you sing with all the voic - es of the

moun - tain? Can you paint with all the col - ors of the wind?___ Can you

paint with all the col - ors of the wind? Come

run the hid - den pine trails of the for - rest, come

124

taste the sun-sweet ber-ries of the earth; come roll in all the rich-es all a-

round you, and for once nev-er won-der what they're worth. The

rain-storm and the riv-er are my bro-thers; the

her-on and the ot-ter are my friends; and

we are all con-nect-ed to each oth-er in a

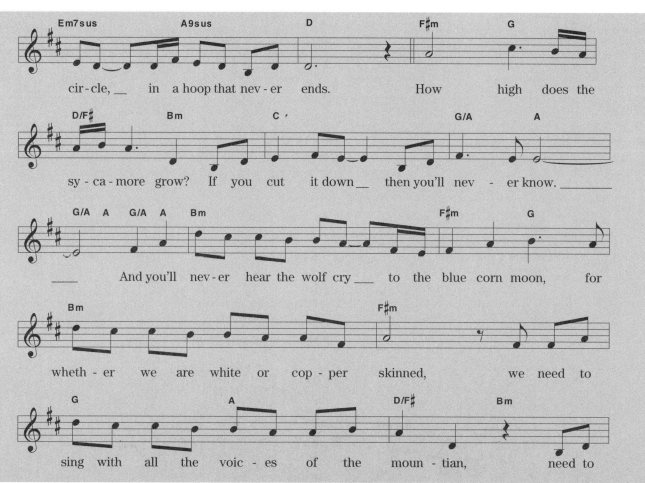

paint with all the col - ors of the wind. You can

own the earth and still all you'll own is earth un - til you can

paint with all the col - ors of the wind.

127